whimsical
FELT
EMBROIDERY

whimsical FELT EMBROIDERY

30 Easy Projects for Creating Exquisite Wall Art

MEGHAN THOMPSON

Founder of Olive & Fox

PAGE STREET
PUBLISHING CO.

First published in 2019 by
Page Street Publishing Co.
27 Congress Street, Suite 105
Salem, MA 01970
www.pagestreetpublishing.com

Distributed by Macmillan, sales in Canada by The Canadian Manda Group.

23   22   21   20   19   1   2   3   4   5

ISBN-13: 978-1-62414-833-0
ISBN-10: 1-62414-833-6

Library of Congress Control Number: 2019932500

Cover and book design by Laura Gallant for Page Street Publishing Co.
Photography by Christopher Thompson
Cover image © Christopher Thompson

Printed and bound in China

Page Street Publishing protects our planet by donating to nonprofits like The Trustees, which focuses on local land conservation.

DEDICATION

To my children, the reason for it all.
Remember, if you can dream it, you can do it.

CONTENTS

Introduction   8

Getting Started   11
Working with Templates   12
Pattern Transfer   12
Felt Template Transfer   13
Tips & Techniques   14
Hooping Your Fabric   14
Threading Your Needle   17
Happy Stitching   18
Beginning a Stitch   18
Ending a Stitch   18
Straight Stitch   18
Running Stitch   19
Backstitch   19
Split Stitch   20
Satin Stitch   20
French Knot   21
Detached Chain Stitch   21
The Finishing Steps   22
Rinsing Your Fabric   22
Finishing Your Hoop   22

The Projects: Embroidered Whimsy for Your Walls   25

The Embroidered Felt Menagerie   27
Llama Love   28
Monkey Business   31
Bee Kind   32
Pretty in Pig   35
Elephant in the Room   36
Love Bug   39
Red Panda-monium   40
Turtle-y Cute   43
Don't Be Jealous Jellyfish   46

Felted Feelings and Whimsy   49
Home Is Wherever I'm with You   50
The Boy Who Lived   53
Adventure Is Calling   56

Make a Splash Mermaid   59
Dino-Roar   60
You Are Loved   63
Oh, the Places You'll Go   64
Spaced Out   67

Felting for Foodies   69

Donut Worry   71
Pizza My Heart   72
Don't Get It Twisted Pretzel   75
Taco to Me   76
Ice Scream, You Scream   79
Love You a Latte   80

Flora and Felt   83

Free Hugs Cactus   85
Monstera Madness   86
Mushroom to Grow   89
Pot of Pilea   90
Fiddle Leaf Figgy with It   93
Sssnake Plant   94
Fresh as a Daisy   97

Make it Personal   98

Name or Custom Text Embroidery   99
Making Faces   100

Tooling Around Tools & Materials   103

Embroidery Hoops   104
Fabrics   105
Felt   105
Embroidery Floss (Thread)   108
Embroidery Needles   108
Straight Pins   109
Water-Soluble Fabric Pens   109
Pencils   109
Rulers   109
Hot Glue Guns   109

Patterns & Felt Templates   110
Acknowledgments   172
About the Author   173
Index   174

INTRODUCTION

When I first started with embroidery, I didn't know that my choice to incorporate felt appliqués would become the defining characteristic of my work and separate my pieces and style from more traditional embroidery work. I love the dimension and texture it brings to a design and the way it slowly brings characters to life with each layer. I soon fell in love with felt: the way its fibers shift and move as I cut it, always keeping me on my toes. Most of all, I love how happy embroidery stitches look when worked through felt.

No matter where you are in your embroidery journey, I want to share this love with you. Whether you've never touched an embroidery needle before or have years of experience with the craft, there's something in here for you.

Beginners will enjoy learning basic embroidery stitches without the pressure or intimidation of a solely embroidered piece. There's a chapter on getting started with embroidery, which walks you through the entire process from cutting your fabric to the final finishing touches. The Tooling Around section (page 103) details everything you will need to complete a project. Take the knowledge you learn here to continue with felt embroidery or venture into more traditional embroidery work.

Intermediate and advanced embroidery artists will enjoy the opportunity to incorporate a new medium into their embroidery work. Adapt the patterns as you see fit: Many of the design elements that are created from felt can be recreated using only embroidery if you prefer a piece with a more heavily embroidered look. Use your embroidery know-how to add custom text or special details to the project.

The beauty of the patterns in this book, and embroidery work in general, is that they allow for so much customization and personalization! These projects are meant to be tailored to your liking—play with the felt, fabric and embroidery floss colors to fit your space. Embroider a name or special phrase on a piece to make a thoughtful and personalized gift for a loved one. Add special embroidered details to a character or animal for a unique piece that's truly one-of-a-kind!

My own love for embroidery work began almost four years ago after the birth of my daughter, Olive. One of the finishing touches to her nursery was a large gallery wall. I was almost finished with the project when I realized something was missing: a unicorn. I don't know if you're like me, but whenever I think whimsical, I think unicorns. And I wanted Olive's room to be a whimsical space that encouraged her imagination to soar! In the same instant I realized a unicorn was needed, I also knew I wanted to make it. I pictured something with texture: a mane you could touch. And in that exact moment, my journey with embroidery began.

Now truth be told, for the embroidered unicorn, the project conception wasn't nearly as difficult as the project realization. I arrived at my local craft store with an image in my mind and not much else. After wandering around the store for quite some time, my mind overwhelmed by choosing the correct needles, fabric and felt, I had the necessary tools to re-create my drawing of a unicorn on a 12-inch (30-cm) embroidery hoop. I was completely intimidated by the thought of embroidering the entire design, and I chose to incorporate felt, figuring I would reserve embroidery work for the unicorn's face and mane. Needless to say, having no previous embroidery experience or pattern to follow, the unicorn project was not without its mishaps and imperfections. Still, the finished piece was whimsical and darling, enough so that my husband encouraged me to open an Etsy shop. And just like that, Olive & Fox was born in March 2015.

Over time, I discovered that embroidery isn't as intimidating as I once thought and that it can even be a relaxing way to unwind after a long day. Now I want to share this enjoyment with you! Let go of the intimidation surrounding embroidery and get stitching! Remember, these patterns are meant to be fun, because felt is a fun fabric! Take your time and work with the proper tools, but don't be afraid to make mistakes. Start over if need be, but just keep embroidering. Wherever you are in your embroidery journey, I hope you enjoy my whimsical and playful felt embroidery!

GETTING STARTED

There's no time like the present to get started with embroidery! In the following section, I will walk you through the process step by step. From pattern transfers to hooping your fabric to making your first stitch, I've got you covered. Visit the Tools & Materials section (page 103) and then get ready to enter the whimsical world of felt embroidery!

Pattern transfer process using a bright window, washi tape and a fabric pen.

Working with Templates

The designs in this book require a combination of both embroidery pattern transfer and felt template transfer. While neither process is particularly difficult, having the correct tools and knowing a few essential tips and techniques will help both processes go more smoothly.

Pattern Transfer

Before you transfer your pattern, cut your fabric to the correct size for your embroidery hoop. Remove your desired pattern from the book using the perforated edge. Lay your fabric right-side up over the pattern. Make sure the pattern is in the correct position under the fabric—some designs will be centered while others will be offset to the sides, top or bottom.

Some fabrics will not require a light source for pattern transfer. But for those that do, hold the pattern and fabric up against a bright window, or if you have one available, a light box. To secure your pattern to the window, place a couple pieces of washi tape on each side. Washi tape does not leave residue behind unlike other types of tape.

Use your marking tool (a water-soluble fabric pen works best, page 109) to trace over the pattern. Don't worry about making mistakes—if you're using a fabric pen, any visible marks will be rinsed out at the end of the project.

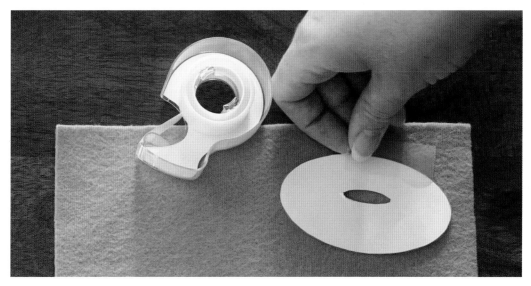

Felt template transfer process using the tape method.

Felt Template Transfer

There are multiple ways to transfer felt templates, but my preferred method for both efficiency and accuracy is the tape method. It's the method I used for each completed project in this book. To begin, you will need to remove your chosen pattern/template page from the book. If the project's instructions call for you to transfer the pattern onto fabric first, do so before you begin the felt template transfer process.

Use a pair of sharp paper scissors to carefully cut out the felt templates in the order given in the instructions. Lay the desired template, printed-side up, down on the felt. Then tape around the perimeter of the template with standard transparent tape, such as Scotch. Be sure not to press down too hard on the tape as it can distort the felt upon removal. The tape holds the template firmly in place while you make your cuts. For additional tips on cutting felt, refer to page 106.

Next, use small fabric scissors to cut around the taped edges of the felt template. When your cuts are complete, gently remove the tape from the felt before positioning it on the hooped fabric. After you remove the tape, you may need to use your fabric scissors to carefully clean up or trim around the edge of the felt piece. Keep in mind that the occasional project may call for you to keep the taped templates on the felt until embroidery begins.

Because of the thickness of felt fabrics, it is almost impossible to transfer a pattern onto felt in the traditional way using a light source. Given that, these patterns will require some freehand drawing on felt, which I've tried to keep relatively simple or at a minimum for those who are not at ease with freehand drawing. Use the included photos for reference, and work with a ruler to determine spacing or straight lines where needed.

When you're done with the templates and patterns, store them in a safe place for future use. I like to store my templates and patterns by project in labeled plastic sandwich or freezer bags, which I keep inside a small storage container. Keeping them grouped by project means I never have to sort through a mix of project templates for the correct ones, which saves me a considerable amount of time.

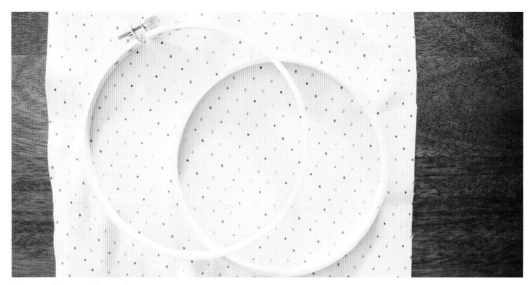

Separated inner and outer hoop rings.

Tips & Techniques

Hooping Your Fabric

Refer to your chosen project for the necessary hoop size. Iron your fabric beforehand to remove any wrinkles that may show or cause distorted stitches. Now cut a square length of your fabric to size, leaving at least 1 to 2 inches (2.5 to 5 cm) of excess fabric. For example, a 6-inch (15-cm) hoop would require at least an 8-inch (20-cm) square of fabric.

Set your cut fabric aside on a clean surface while you separate the inner ring of the hoop from the outer ring by unscrewing it at the top. Lay the fabric square centered over the inner ring on a clean, hard surface. Make sure the horizontal and vertical weave of the fabric is straightly aligned before you place the outer ring on top of the fabric. Gently press down on the outer ring to secure the fabric in between the inner and outer ring. The screw on the outer ring should be at the top of your fabric. Tighten the screw a little before you adjust the fabric into place.

To adjust the fabric, first pull gently on the left-hand side and then pull gently on the right-hand side. As you adjust the fabric, pay close attention to the horizontal and vertical weave of the fabric. Both weaves should look straight without being overly distorted. Minor distortion is to be expected. Pull gently on the top and bottom of the fabric, being mindful of the weave. Pulling on the fabric ensures a snug, but not too tight, fit of fabric to the hoop without any wrinkles or loose material. It's important to get the fabric neatly and snugly into place, without being too loose or taut, as either could create warped embroidery stitches. Take your time and start over if needed. When your fabric is in the desired position, tighten the outer ring's screw to ensure the fabric will hold in place while you embroider.

When your fabric is in the correct position, you are ready to remove any excess fabric that may get in your way during embroidery. You can leave your fabric in the square shape or cut along the rounded lines of the hoop. Be sure to leave at least 1 inch (2.5 cm) of excess fabric for closing the hoop at the end of the project.

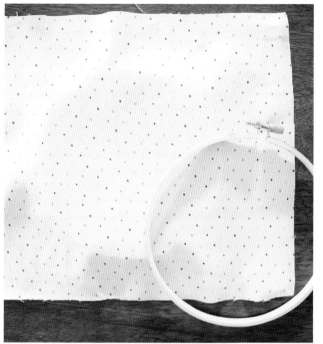

Lay the fabric square over the inner ring of the hoop.

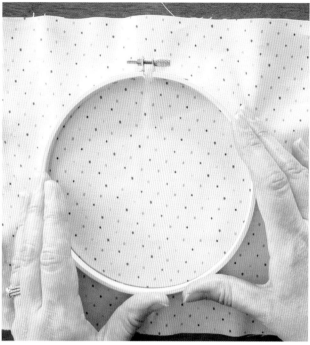

Gently press down on the outer ring to secure the fabric between both rings.

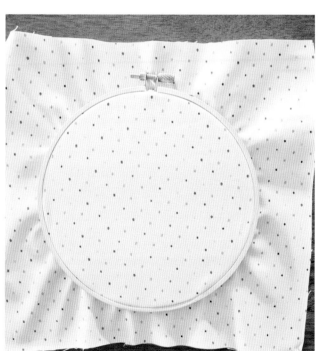

Now you're ready to adjust the fabric.

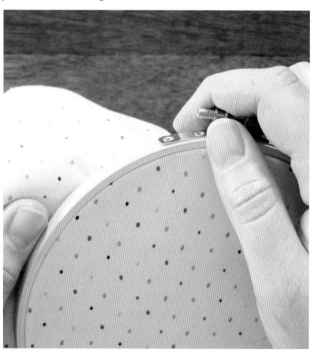

Pull gently on the fabric starting on the top left-hand side.

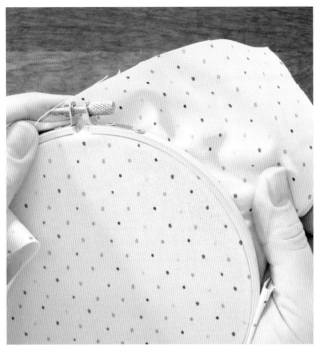

Next, pull gently on the right-hand side of the fabric.

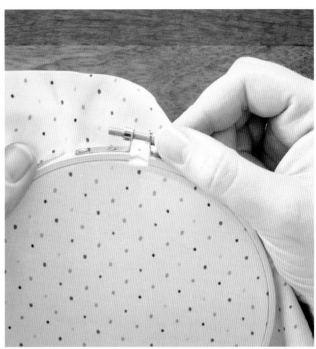

Once your fabric is in the desired position, finish tightening the screw.

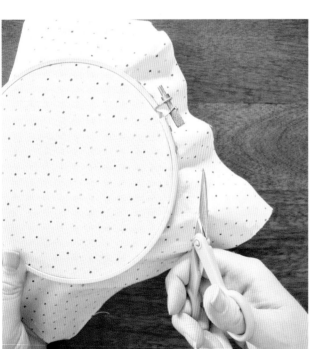

Remove the excess fabric.

Be sure to leave at least 1 inch (2.5 cm) of excess fabric.

Pull the embroidery floss through the eye of the needle.

Threading Your Needle

Start by cutting approximately 20 inches (51 cm) of embroidery floss from the skein. Use sharp fabric scissors to ensure a clean cut. Before you thread your embroidery needle, read the project's instructions to determine how many strands of embroidery floss are required for that particular embroidery step. Embroidery floss consists of six strands of cotton floss. Some instructions may call for you to separate out anywhere from one to five strands of floss for smaller, finer details (page 108). Separate the required strands before threading your needle.

To thread your needle, grab one end of the floss (thread) between your thumb and forefinger of your dominant hand. Poke the floss through the circular end of the needle (the eye). Sometimes wetting the very end of the thread with your mouth helps to poke the strands through. Pull the floss through the eye at least 3 inches (8 cm) to keep the floss securely on the needle while you embroider. Next, tie a knot in the opposite end of the floss, approximately ½ to 1 inch (1.3 to 2.5 cm) from the end; this ensures that your floss does not pull through the fabric on your first stitch. When your needle is threaded, you are ready to make your first stitch!

Happy Stitching

There are numerous types of embroidery stitches—ranging from easy to complex. Indeed, one of the joys and challenges of embroidery is that there are always new stitching techniques or adaptations to learn.

The embroidery stitches featured in this section are ones that are needed to complete the projects in this book. These stitches are perfect for those new to embroidery, and they are great for those who are looking to practice and improve upon their embroidery skills while incorporating a new medium, like felt, into their work. More experienced embroidery artists may enjoy substituting some stitches outlined in these patterns with more advanced techniques wherever they see fit.

Beginning a Stitch

Using the thumb and forefinger of your dominant hand to hold the needle, with your other hand holding the hoop, insert your needle through the backside of the fabric at your selected starting point. Reach around the front of the hoop and grab the needle with your dominant hand. Pull the embroidery thread all the way through until the knotted end of the thread gently bumps up against the back of the fabric.

When the knotted end has reached the back of the fabric, you are ready to work your first stitch!

Ending a Stitch

Ending a stitch is common throughout the course of an embroidery project. You will end a stitch whenever you've completed an embroidery section, need to switch thread colors or run out of thread.

There are several different techniques for ending a stitch. Perhaps one of the simplest methods is the knot method. When it is time to end a stitch, reserve at least 3 inches (8 cm) of floss to make a knot. If you leave less than 3 inches (8 cm), you may have difficulties making a knot with the floss, which can be very frustrating!

When you are coming to the end of your thread or need to switch floss colors, unthread your needle and simply make a knot in the floss after your last stitch. The knot should rest against the back of the fabric to prevent your last stitch from moving. Use your fabric scissors to snip the excess floss from the knot, but be careful not to accidentally snip the knot itself. I typically leave ¼ inch (6 mm) of thread after the knot, which is short enough so that the tail end of the knot can't be seen through the fabric but doesn't risk the knot coming loose and unraveling.

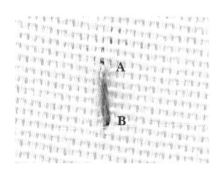

Straight Stitch

The straight stitch is the most basic of stitches. It involves bringing the needle up through the back of the fabric (A) and back down again in one single stitch (B). While simple, the straight stitch can be used as the foundation for other stitches, such as a straight flower or star. The straight stitch is used throughout the book whenever one stitch is required or sporadic, randomly placed stitches are needed, such as the sprinkles on a donut or the pattern on a plant.

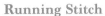

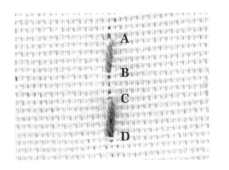

Running Stitch

The running stitch is one of the most basic stitches. It works well for making dashed outlines, and despite being the first stitch I learned, I continue to use it in my patterns to embroider along the perimeter of designs, fully securing the felt piece to the fabric.

To make a running stitch, poke your needle up through the back of the fabric at your starting point (A). Depending on the desired length of your running stitches, poke the needle back down through the fabric a short distance (B) from the starting point and pull the floss down through the fabric, creating your first straight stitch.

Now, leaving a space in the fabric between your next stitch and the previous stitch, poke your needle back up through the fabric (C) and then back down through the fabric (D). Repeat this sequence until you complete the running stitch portion of the instructions.

Work with an even tension, and be careful not to pull the floss too hard or the fabric will pucker between your stitches.

Focus on making your stitches even in length and spacing. The amount of space between the stitches can be the same length as the stitches themselves or shorter/longer for design purposes. Whichever length you choose, keep it consistent through that section of embroidery. For my outlining purposes, I often make my running stitches approximately ⅛ inch (3 mm) in length while the space between the stitches may vary from project to project.

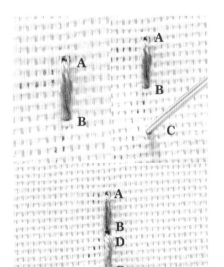

Backstitch

The backstitch is a versatile, basic stitch that gets its name from the direction you stitch it in. It's useful for outlining, embroidering straight and curved lines and for creating text. It will be used throughout the patterns in this book for those purposes.

To work a backstitch, begin by making one forward straight stitch: Poke your needle up through the back of the fabric at your starting point (A). Bring your needle back down a short distance from your starting point, making one forward straight stitch (B). From the back of the fabric, space the needle out the desired length of your stitch and poke up through the backside of the fabric (C). Now bring the needle and floss back down through the fabric at the end of the previous stitch (D). Repeat this sequence until you complete the backstitch section of the pattern.

Work with an even tension to avoid puckering your fabric. If you are new to the backstitch, you may want to mark your spacing with a fabric pen (page 109) to help achieve evenly spaced stitches.

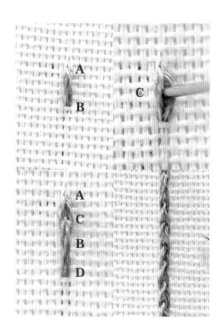

Split Stitch

The split stitch is similar to the backstitch in that it makes a solid line and it can be used for outlining or embroidering straight or curved lines. I like to work with the split stitch whenever I want to create a braided or woven-like texture, and you will see it employed here for those purposes.

To make a split stitch, start by poking your needle through the back side of the fabric at your starting point (A). Bring your needle and floss back down through the front of the fabric to make one straight stitch (B). Next, pull your needle back up through the underside of your fabric in the center of your previous stitch, splitting the strands of floss down the center (C). Then use your needle to make another straight stitch the exact same length as your first straight stitch (D). Repeat this sequence throughout the split stitch section of the design.

Depending on whether you are creating a straight or curved line, adjust the length of your split stitches. Short split stitches tend to work best for curved lines while either long or short stitches work for straight lines.

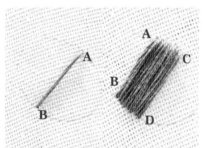

Satin Stitch

The satin stitch is a classic embroidery stitch that's perfect for filling in shapes. I frequently use it in my designs to fill in details such as an animal's inner ears or flower petals. Satin stitches can also be used to fill in thick, bold letters in text, such as in the Donut Worry pattern (page 71).

Begin by using your fabric pen to outline the shape or text you'd like to fill. The outline provides a useful guide for your satin stitches. To work a satin stitch, bring your needle and floss up through the fabric at your starting point (A). Then bring it down through the fabric directly across from where you started on the opposite side of the shape (B). Basically, you are creating a series of straight stitches that run back and forth from one end of the shape to the other. Poke the needle back up again on the side where you started (C), and go back down again on the opposite side of shape (D) creating another straight stitch. Repeat the sequence until you have filled in the outlined shape entirely.

As you work a satin stitch, be sure to keep your floss strands straight and not twisted. As always, work with even tension and take special care not to pull the floss too tight or it will create fabric puckers. If you are using the satin stitch for filling text, I recommend knotting off your floss and cutting it before starting the next letter to avoid pulling and puckering of the fabric between letters.

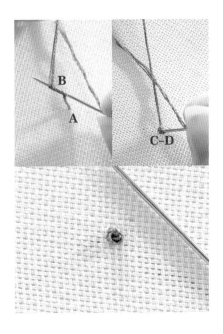

French Knot

The French knot is another classic stitch that I favor for its versatility. Some of my uses for a French knot stitch include floral designs, and buttons, eyes and other accessories for character designs. In addition to accent work, it is well-suited for filler work. The French knot can be a bit difficult to master at first, but like with any stitch, practice is key. After all, the French knot's versatility makes it well worth the effort and time.

The French knot stitch requires two hands. Begin by bringing your needle up through the back of the fabric (A). Now wrap the floss around your needle two or three times (B). While holding the end of the floss taut, but not too tight, bring the needle back down next to your original entry point (C). Continue to hold the floss taut as you bring the needle all the way through the fabric (D).

Feel free to increase or decrease the size of your French knot by varying the amount of times you wrap the floss around the needle (B). Wrapping the floss once will give you a smaller knot, while three times around achieves a larger French knot.

Because French knots can be very tricky to unknot and typically require cutting to remove from your work, I recommend beginning a new section of floss every time you make a French knot while you are learning. Too many times I've made three or four knots in a row only to have to cut them all out and start again when one doesn't knot well.

Detached Chain Stitch

This looped embroidery stitch is a favorite of mine for creating flowers, leaves or other fun accents, such as the hair at the end of an elephant's tail (Elephant in the Room, page 36).

To work a detached chain stitch, begin by bringing your needle up through the fabric at your starting point (A). Bring your needle back down through the fabric as if making a straight stitch, but do not pull your needle and floss all the way through the fabric. Instead, allow the floss to form a loop shape (B). Now bring the needle up through the inside of the loop toward the top where the loop curves (C). Make a small stitch over the top of the loop, securing the loop in place (D). Repeat this sequence as many times as the instructions note.

Embroidering five or six detached chain stitches in a circle will create a lazy daisy flower, which looks sweet when finished with a French knot in the center of the looped petals.

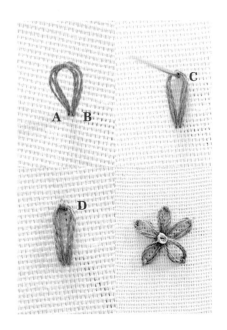

The Finishing Steps

Much like beginning your hoop, the steps for finishing your project are relatively simple, but they require practice and patience when you're first beginning with embroidery.

Rinsing Your Fabric

If you used a water-soluble fabric pen (page 109) to mark the design, you will need to rinse and dry your fabric before you can close your hoop. Be sure to fully read the instructions on your fabric pen packaging before you begin the rinsing process.

Before you rinse your finished design, prepare a clean, hard surface for your fabric to dry. Remove the fabric from the hoop. Hold your design under a slow-running faucet to rinse it. Blotting at the pen marks with a cloth may cause them to temporarily disappear but they may reappear as the fabric dries. In order to prevent the pen marks from reappearing, fully rinse your design. When the rinsing is complete, lay your fabric flat to dry. Gently smooth out any wrinkles in the fabric and the felt before it dries.

When your fabric and felt are fully dry, you may put the fabric back on the hoop unless you are going to add a fabric backing, which I recommend to protect your embroidery work. When testing your fabric for dryness, pay particular attention to the felt portions of your design as they may take longer to dry. When the fabric and felt are dry, you are ready to finish your hoop!

Finishing Your Hoop

There are a variety of ways to finish your hoop. The method I describe here is a relatively simple process that I use for many of my embroidery projects. For this method, you will need:

- Fabric for the back of the hoop (see below)

- Fabric scissors

- Hot glue gun with glue sticks

1. Cut a square length of your backing fabric to size, approximately 1 to 2 inches (2.5 to 5 cm) larger than your hoop size (see photo on page 15). For example, a 6-inch (15-cm) hoop would require a 7- to 8-inch (18- to 20-cm) square cut length of your backing fabric. When selecting fabric for backing, I like to use the same fabric I used in the design, as long as it's not a patterned fabric, or I use a solid, cotton fabric in a lighter color than the front fabric. I avoid using patterned fabrics for the backing, as they often show through the front of the hoop. White cotton quilting fabric makes a good choice for most backings.

2. Iron your backing fabric to remove any excess wrinkles.

3. Lay your cut square of backing fabric over the inner ring of the hoop. Smooth out any wrinkles in the backing fabric with your hand before laying your completed design over it. Place the fabric with your finished embroidery work over the backing fabric. Again, smooth out any wrinkles in the top fabric with your hand. Next, take the outer ring of the hoop and place it over the completed work with the backing fabric and inner ring underneath. As you are aligning the outer ring to place it over the fabrics and inner ring, pay particular attention to how you want the design to lay in the outer hoop (e.g., centered, offset, etc.). The tightening screw should be centered at the top of your hoop. Gently press down on the outer ring to secure the fabrics and inner ring inside of the outer ring.

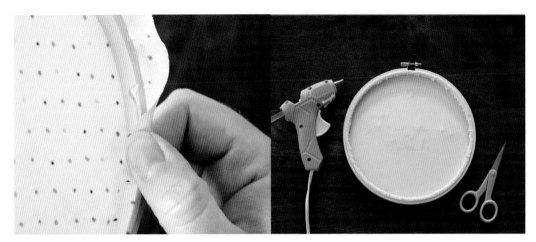

Gluing fabric to the inner hoop.   *The back of a complete project.*

4.   Now, working in the same left-to-right, top-to-bottom order as when you originally hooped your fabric, pull on the two layers of fabric to remove any wrinkles. Be mindful of the horizontal and vertical weaves of your top fabric to avoid distortions. Turn your hoop over to examine the backing fabric. I like both my top and backing fabric to be free of wrinkles, so I smooth them by gently pulling on the fabric before I flip the hoop over again and resume smoothing out wrinkles from the front.

5.   When you have smoothed out the wrinkles, checked the weave of the top fabric and ensured that your design is placed to your liking inside the outer ring, tighten the screws to secure the fabrics and inner ring into place. Now you are ready to trim the excess fabric from the backing fabric.

6.   Flip the hoop over so the back is facing up. Separate the two layers of fabric with your fingers to ensure that you do not accidentally cut the top fabric with your completed embroidery work. Use your fabric scissors to cut along the base of the inner hoop where the backing fabric meets the hoop. Do not worry about cutting the backing fabric all the way down to the inner hoop; just cut it as close as you comfortably can around the entire length of the hoop. Discard the excess backing fabric.

7.   Next, you may cut the excess fabric from the top fabric. Remember to leave at least ¼ inch (6 mm) of fabric around the entire length of the hoop as you will use that to hot glue the fabric into place on the inner hoop.

8.   After you've finished cutting the top fabric, you are ready to hot glue it to the inner ring. Allow your hot glue gun to fully heat before gluing the fabric. Test the glue on a heat-safe surface before proceeding. Please note that if you'd prefer not to work with hot glue, you can use the same technique with fabric glue, although you will need to adjust for a longer setting and drying time.

9.   Now that the hot glue is fully heated, you are ready to proceed. I like to start at the top center of the hoop where the tightening screw is located and work my way around. Working in small sections, hot glue a section of the top of the inner hoop, not the sides, and press the excess ¼ inch (6 mm) of fabric into the glue. Gluing on the top of the inner hoop rather than the sides helps prevent the glue from getting on the back of your finished work.

10. Use caution when working with hot glue. It dries quickly, so you will need to work quickly. Work in small sections to avoid the glue drying before you can press the fabric into place. When you have glued the excess fabric around the entire inner hoop, your project is complete!

the projects

EMBROIDERED WHIMSY FOR YOUR WALLS

the embroidered
FELT
MENAGERIE

As a lifelong animal lover and pet owner, animal embroidery is some of my favorite to design and create. In fact, some of my earliest work was inspired by sloths, swans and bears . . . oh my!

The beauty of making these designs is that they typically call for you to layer multiple pieces of felt to give the animals dimension and character. As you layer each piece of felt on the design, you'll notice how the animal comes to life on your hoop. Some of my favorite projects in this chapter, Monkey Business (page 31), Llama Love (page 28) and Pretty in Pig (page 35), are perfect examples of the added fun and whimsy each layer of felt brings to embroidery! Adding facial features, fur or special details, such as a bow tie, further bring the piece to life. They also encourage you to sample a variety of stitches to achieve the desired look.

Luckily for beginners, most of the designs in this chapter can be created with the knowledge of just a few stitches, like the running stitch, backstitch and satin stitch. More experienced stitchers will enjoy using additional embroidery techniques to add those special touches, such as elaborate flower crowns, to personalize the design.

LLAMA LOVE

Llamas get a lot of love in home décor, and it's no wonder why with their shaggy coats and charming faces. And just as one would expect, embroidering a llama is quite fun. Choose from a variety of neutral felts to create your llama's body, face and ears, and then go wild choosing bright felt pieces to create the llama's decorative rug. Have fun using the split stitch and French knots in creative ways to add special details to your llama's reins and rug! Make several llama hoops for a colorful herd to brighten your home!

Patterns/Templates: page 111

Stitches: Running stitch (page 19), backstitch (page 19), satin stitch (page 20), split stitch (page 20) and French knot (page 21)

Hoop size: 7-inch (18-cm) round

Fabric: 9-inch (23-cm) square of fabric (navy blue)

Felt colors: White, cream, turquoise, pink and coral

Embroidery floss colors: Ecru, white, dark brown, yellow, pink, dark coral, coral and turquoise

Other materials: Fabric scissors, paper scissors, regular adhesive tape, straight pins, embroidery needle, water-soluble fabric pen and ruler

Hoop the fabric and trim the excess, leaving at least 1 inch (2.5 cm) of excess around the entire hoop.

Template Transfer and Felt Fabric Instructions

1. Transfer the llama template (#1) onto the white felt. Secure the felt llama to the hoop fabric with straight pins.

2. Transfer the llama's ears (#3) onto the cream felt. Place them at the top of the llama's head with the llama's head slightly overlapping the bottom of the ears. Pin both ears and use two strands of ecru embroidery floss to running stitch them into place.

3. Stitch the llama body into place, with three strands of white floss, using a running stitch.

4. Transfer the llama face template (#2) onto the cream felt. Use a straight pin to hold the cream face in place on the llama while you running stitch along the perimeter of the face using two strands of ecru floss.

5. Next, transfer the llama's hair tuft template (#4) onto the white felt. Position it into place at the top of the head, overlapping the top of the llama's face and centered between both ears. Use a running stitch with two strands of white floss to stitch it.

6. To make the decorative rug, transfer template #5 onto the turquoise felt. Pin it into place on the llama's back. Transfer template #6 onto the pink felt and pin it on top of the turquoise felt. Finally, transfer template #7 onto the coral felt. Pin the coral piece on top of the pink felt.

Embroidery Instructions

1. Begin by using your fabric pen to draw the llama's face. Use a ruler to center the llama's eyes, mouth and nose. For the nose and mouth, draw a vertical oval shape centered in the middle of the face. Next, draw the nose at the top of the oval. The nose is shaped like an upside-down triangle. Now use your pen to draw a straight line down from the "point" of the upside-down triangle, creating the llama's mouth. Use two strands of dark brown embroidery floss to embroider with a backstitch over your marked face lines. Reserve the remaining four strands of dark brown floss for the llama's hooves.

2. To embroider the hooves, use the remaining four strands of dark brown floss to satin stitch in the hooves over the white felt of the llama's feet where it's tapered at the bottom. Each hoof is a little under ½ inch (1.3 cm) in height.

3. For the decorative rug, use four strands of yellow embroidery floss to split stitch along the perimeter of the turquoise, pink and coral felt pieces. To complete the rug's look, use six strands of the dark coral floss to embroider eleven French knots along the bottom of the turquoise felt. If needed, use your fabric pen to mark out the French knot placement.

4. For the reins, start by marking their placement with your fabric pen. Embroider over your marked lines with six strands of yellow floss using a split stitch. Using alternating floss colors of pink, dark coral, coral and turquoise, embroider French knots under each of the yellow reins.

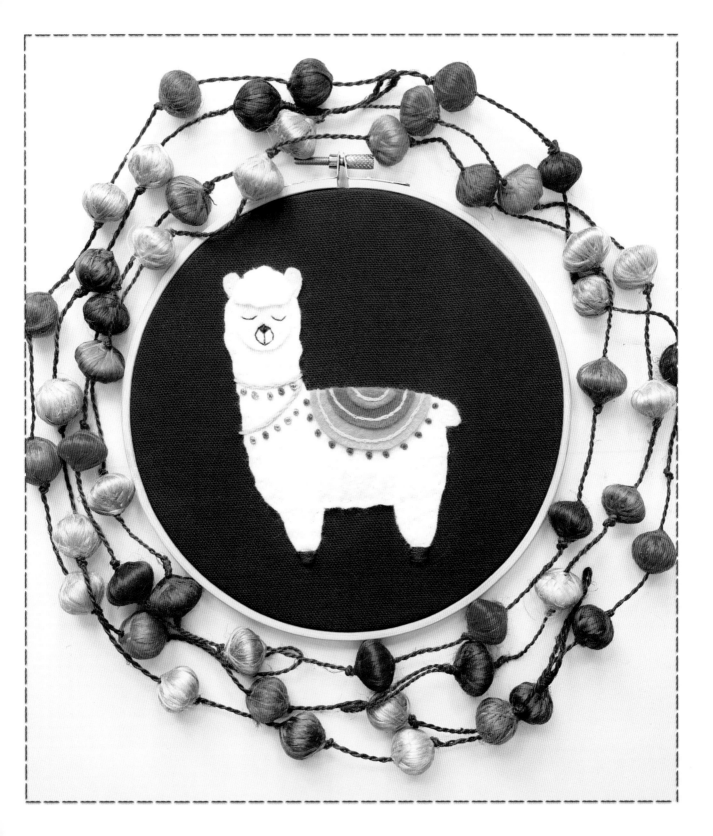

MONKEY BUSINESS

This design was inspired by my family's trips to the local zoos to visit our favorite monkeys. With about 260 known monkey species in the world, there's truly a favorite for everyone! This monkey pattern clearly falls into the "adorable monkey" variety, and it would look right at home in a zoo-inspired nursery or an animal lover's bedroom or play area. The layering of multiple embroidered felt pieces gives this sweet monkey lots of character!

Patterns/Templates: page 113

Stitches: Running stitch (page 19), backstitch (page 19), satin stitch (page 20) and detached chain stitch (page 21)

Hoop size: 8-inch (20-cm) round

Fabric: 9-inch (23-cm) square of fabric (mint)

Felt colors: Brown and tan

Embroidery floss colors: Brown, tan, black and light peach

Other materials: Fabric scissors, paper scissors, regular adhesive tape, straight pins, embroidery needle and water-soluble fabric pen

Hoop the fabric and trim the excess, leaving at least 1 inch (2.5 cm) excess around the entire hoop.

Template Transfer and Felt Fabric Instructions

1. Transfer the monkey head template (#1) onto the brown felt fabric. Next, secure the brown felt monkey head to the hoop fabric by placing a straight pin in each ear and two pins in the main portion of the head. When placing the monkey head on the fabric, be sure to leave space at the bottom of the hoop if you wish to add a name or custom text embroidery (page 99).

2. Stitch the monkey head into place, with six strands of brown embroidery floss, using a running stitch. Remove the pins.

3. Transfer the monkey face template (#2) onto the tan felt fabric. Use straight pins to pin the tan felt monkey face into place on the brown monkey head.

4. Next, with six strands of tan thread, work a running stitch to secure the monkey face into place on top of the monkey head. Remove the pins.

5. Transfer the monkey mouth template (#3) onto the leftover tan felt. Pin the monkey mouth into place on the monkey head, slightly overlapping the monkey's eyes but not overlapping the monkey's ears, with straight pins.

6. Work a running stitch, with six strands of the tan floss, to stitch the monkey mouth into place. Remove the pins.

Embroidery Instructions

1. First use your fabric pen to mark the monkey's eyes, nostrils, mouth, cheeks and inner ears on the felt. Use the Monkey Business picture on the previous page for placement references. Add two to three eyelashes at the outer corner of each eye if desired. With a backstitch, use four strands of black embroidery floss to stitch over your pen marks and along the monkey's eyes and mouth. Next, use a satin stitch to fill in the monkey's nostrils with the four strands of black thread.

2. Switching to four strands of the light peach floss, satin stitch the monkey's cheeks and inner ears.

3. For the monkey's hair, use six strands of brown thread to make three detached chain stitches, slightly overlapping at the bottom of the stitch, at the top of his head.

BEE KIND

A friendly little bee buzzes by to remind us that kindness is always the best choice. This design uses four different stitches and just two embroidery floss colors to create a simple and sweet message for your home.

Patterns/Templates: page 115

Stitches: Running stitch (page 19), backstitch (page 19), French knot (page 21) and straight stitch (page 18)

Hoop size: 6-inch (15-cm) round

Fabric: 8-inch (20-cm) square of fabric (white)

Felt colors: Light yellow, white and black

Embroidery floss colors: Black and light yellow

Other materials: Water-soluble fabric pen, fabric scissors, paper scissors, regular adhesive tape, straight pins and embroidery needle

Transfer the text pattern onto your fabric. Hoop the fabric and trim the excess, leaving at least 1 inch (2.5 cm) excess around the entire hoop.

Text Embroidery Instructions

1. Begin by using a running stitch with four strands of black embroidery floss to embroider over the looped lines.

2. Starting with the letter K, switch to a backstitch with four strands of black floss to embroider the word *Kind*. Use a French knot to make the dot over the letter i.

Felt Template Transfer and Embroidery Instructions

1. Start by transferring the bee body template (#1) onto the light yellow felt and secure it into place. The bee's stinger should end where the black running stitch of the looped line begins.

2. Transfer the bee's wings (#2) onto the white felt fabric. Pin it into place above the bee's body with the body slightly overlapping the bottom of the wings. Use two strands of black floss to backstitch along the perimeter of the wings. Make a straight stitch in the center of both wings with the black floss.

3. When the wings are embroidered into place, use a running stitch with three strands of the light yellow floss to embroider along the perimeter of the bee's body.

4. Transfer the bee's stripes (#3) onto the black felt. Pin the stripes into place on the bee's body. With three strands of black embroidery floss, use a running stitch to secure the stripes onto the body.

5. To complete the bee, use four strands of black embroidery floss to embroider the facial features and legs. With a French knot, embroider the bee's eye. Next, use two curved straight stitches with the black floss to create the bee's smiling mouth. Finally, make four vertical straight stitches under the bee's body for the legs.

PRETTY IN PIG

To quote the delightful children's book, Charlotte's Web, *this is "some pig"! For this project, I decided to fully embrace my love of the color pink. Layer shades of blush-tone felts together to create a truly adorable pig. And just when you think she couldn't possibly get any cuter, you'll stitch the finishing touches on her darling felt flower crown. Prepare to squeal with delight!*

Patterns/Templates: page 117

Stitches: Running stitch (page 19), backstitch (page 19), French knot (page 21) and straight stitch (page 18)

Hoop size: 6-inch (15-cm) round

Fabric: 8-inch (20-cm) square of fabric (pink and white plaid)

Felt colors: Oat, blush, white and olive-green

Embroidery floss colors: Very light desert sand, medium desert sand, dark olive-green, cranberry and black

Other materials: Fabric scissors, paper scissors, regular adhesive tape, straight pins, ruler, embroidery needle and water-soluble fabric pen

Hoop the fabric and trim the excess, leaving at least 1 inch (2.5 cm) excess around the entire hoop.

Template Transfer and Felt Fabric Instructions

1. Transfer the pig head template (#1) onto the oat-colored felt fabric and secure it with straight pins. When placing the pig head onto the fabric, be sure to leave space at the bottom of the hoop if you wish to add a name or custom text embroidery (page 99). Embroider a running stitch using three strands of the very light desert sand thread around the perimeter of the head.

2. Transfer the pig snout template (#2) onto the blush felt fabric, and pin it towards the bottom-center of the pig's head. Use a ruler to ensure that the snout is centered before embroidering along the outline of the snout with two strands of medium desert sand thread in a backstitch.

3. Transfer the pig's cheek templates (#3) onto the blush felt. Pin a cheek on both sides of the snout. Work a backstitch with two strands of medium desert sand floss along the border of each cheek.

4. For the pig's flower crown, transfer the flower template (#4) onto the white felt and the leaves template (#5) onto the olive-green felt. The felt leaves piece should be pinned at the top of the pig's head running diagonally next to the right ear. Use a backstitch with two strands of dark olive-green thread to embroider a center "vein" running across the center of the leaves, securing the felt leaves to the pig. Lay the flower over the center of the leaves with the two leaves poking out from both sides of the flower. With six strands of cranberry floss, embroider a series of French knots in the center of the flower to secure it in place.

Embroidery Instructions

1. First use your fabric pen to mark the pig's eyes. Use the Pretty in Pig picture on the previous page for placement references. The eyes should be centered above the cheeks and snout. With a backstitch, use three strands of black embroidery floss to stitch the eyes. Add two eyelashes to both eyes using a straight stitch for the bottom lashes and two curved backstitches for the upper.

2. For the pig's nostrils, draw two small circles towards the top of the snout. Use your ruler to ensure the nostrils are equal distance from the sides of the snout. Embroider a French knot with six strands of medium desert sand thread for both of the nostrils.

ELEPHANT IN THE ROOM

Elephants are majestic creatures, no doubt about it. This felt elephant is treated like royalty on a rich purple fabric with regal French knot accents. Display your elephant embroidery on its own, or pair it with the Llama Love hoop (page 28) for an extra-colorful display!

Patterns/Templates: page 119

Stitches: Running stitch (page 19), backstitch (page 19), satin stitch (page 20), split stitch (page 20), French knot (page 21), straight stitch (page 18) and detached chain stitch (page 21)

Hoop size: 7-inch (18-cm) round

Fabric: 9-inch (23-cm) square of fabric (purple with navy and black pattern)

Felt colors: Light gray, purple, lavender and turquoise

Embroidery floss colors: Light gray, black, white, mint, purple and lavender

Other materials: Fabric scissors, paper scissors, regular adhesive tape, straight pins, embroidery needle and water-soluble fabric pen

Hoop the fabric and trim the excess, leaving at least 1 inch (2.5 cm) excess around the entire hoop.

Template Transfer and Felt Fabric Instructions

1. Transfer the elephant template (#1) onto the light gray felt fabric. Pin the felt elephant to the hoop fabric and embroider it into place with a running stitch using four strands of light gray embroidery floss.

2. Transfer the elephant ear template (#2) onto the light gray felt. Secure the ear on the elephant's head. Embroider it along the perimeter using a running stitch with four strands of light gray floss.

3. To make the decorative rug on the elephant's back, begin by transferring template #3 onto the purple felt. Pin it into place on the elephant's back. Transfer template #4 onto the lavender felt, and pin it on top of the purple felt. Lastly, transfer template #5 onto the turquoise felt. Pin the turquoise felt onto the top of the lavender felt.

Embroidery Instructions

1. Begin by using your fabric pen to draw the elephant's eye. Embroider the eye using three strands of black embroidery floss with a backstitch.

2. To embroider the elephant's toenails, start by outlining them with your fabric pen. Use three strands of white embroidery floss to satin stitch in the nails. Satin stitch the center, longest stitch of each nail first and fill in the sides next.

3. For the decorative rug, use four strands of mint embroidery floss to split stitch along the perimeter of the purple, lavender and turquoise felt pieces. To complete the rug's look, use six strands of the mint floss to embroider seven French knots along the bottom of the purple felt. If needed, use your fabric pen to mark out the French knot placement. Make a small vertical straight stitch with the mint floss under each of the French knots.

4. To embroider the elephant's decorative headress on its forehead, start by marking the placement with your fabric pen. Embroider over the marked line with a split stitch using six strands of mint embroidery floss. Make a total of four French knots under the split stitch, alternating purple and lavender embroidery floss. Use the corresponding floss color to make a small vertical straight stitch under each of the knots.

5. The final step is to embroider the elephant's tail. Begin by marking the elephant's tail with your fabric pen. Use four strands of light gray embroidery floss to backstitch over your tail line. Lastly, make three detached chain stitches at the end of the tail. Stitch the center detached chain first with the two side detached chain stitches fanning out from the center detached chain.

LOVE BUG

This Love Bug design was inspired by my daughter, who loves ladybugs and the color pink! This little bug would look adorable "crawling" along the walls of any nursery or kid's room. You can customize this piece by using different colors of felt or embroidery floss to create the bug's body and spots. And the customization options don't stop there! Fill in the bug's spots with a satin stitch, as shown, or use the included spot template to cut them from felt. After all, no two "love bugs" are alike!

Patterns/Templates: page 121

Stitches: Running stitch (page 19), backstitch (page 19), satin stitch (page 20), straight stitch (page 18) and French knot (page 21)

Hoop size: 6-inch (15-cm) round

Fabric: 8-inch (20-cm) square of fabric (ivory with pink polka dots)

Felt colors: Pink and black

Embroidery floss colors: Pink, black and white

Other materials: Fabric scissors, paper scissors, regular adhesive tape, straight pins, embroidery needle, water-soluble fabric pen, ruler and white chalk

Hoop the fabric and trim the excess, leaving at least 1 inch (2.5 cm) excess around the entire hoop.

Template Transfer and Felt Fabric Instructions

1. Transfer the bug body template (#2) onto the pink felt fabric. Next, secure the pink felt body to the hoop fabric with two straight pins.

2. Stitch the bug body into place with the pink embroidery floss, using a running stitch. Remove the pins.

3. Transfer the bug head template (#1) onto the black felt fabric. Use a straight pin to hold the black felt bug head into place on the fabric directly above the pink bug body. Be sure that both pieces line up and touch with no space in between them.

4. Next, with the black embroidery floss, use a running stitch to secure the head into place.

Embroidery Instructions

1. First, with a ruler, use your fabric pen to draw the center "wing" line running down the bug's back. Use the Love Bug picture on the previous page for placement references. Work a backstitch with three strands of black floss over the traced line. Next, use the small circle templates (#3) to trace out the spots on the bug's back with your fabric pen. Different species of ladybugs have different numbers of spots, so feel free to play around with your spot count and placement. Fill in each spot using a satin stitch with three strands of black embroidery floss. For spots that really pop, use the spot template to transfer the spots onto the felt. Embroider the spots into place on the bug's back using one or two straight stitches.

2. For the legs and antennae, use your fabric pen to mark the placement of them. As shown in the picture, the legs are approximately ¾ inch (2 cm) apart on both sides. With three strands of your black embroidery floss, use a backstitch to embroider over the legs and antennae. Work a French knot of six strands of black floss at the end of both antennae to complete the look.

3. For the bug's face, use a piece of slim white chalk to mark the placement of the bug's eyes and cheeks. Embroider the eyes with three strands of white embroidery floss using a backstitch. Stitch in eyelashes at the corner of each eye if desired. Next, use three strands of white floss to satin stitch in the cheeks.

Text Embroidery Instructions

1. Remove the fabric from the hoop to transfer the Love Bug text onto your fabric. Use the Love Bug picture on the previous page for a text placement reference. Feel free to place the text in your own desired location or omit the text completely from the design. When the text is transferred and the fabric is back on the hoop, use two strands of the black embroidery floss to backstitch the letters.

RED PANDA-MONIUM

I'd be hard-pressed to think of an animal much cuter than the red panda. Their beautiful cinnamon-colored fur and distinctive facial markings make them a perfect subject for felt embroidery. Watch how the layers of white and black felt on the cinnamon head bring your red panda to life! This sweet panda would look especially cute with a little bow tie or perhaps a flower crown for those looking for an additional embroidery challenge. Use the tips for adding name embroidery (page 99) to personalize this piece.

Patterns/Templates: page 123

Stitches: Running stitch (page 19), backstitch (page 19) and straight stitch (page 18)

Hoop size: 7-inch (18-cm) round

Fabric: 9-inch (23-cm) square of fabric (teal with purple wood grain pattern)

Felt colors: Cinnamon, white and black

Embroidery floss colors: White, dark burnt orange and black

Other materials: Fabric scissors, paper scissors, regular adhesive tape, straight pins, embroidery needle, ruler and water-soluble fabric pen

Hoop the fabric and trim the excess, leaving at least 1 inch (2.5 cm) excess around the entire hoop.

Template Transfer and Felt Fabric Instructions

1. Transfer the red panda template (#1) onto the cinnamon-colored felt fabric and secure it with straight pins. Wait to embroider the head until you stitch the ears into place. When placing the red panda head on the fabric, be sure to leave space at the bottom of the hoop if you wish to add a name or custom text embroidery (page 99).

2. Transfer the ear templates (#6) onto the white felt fabric, and pin both ears at the top of the red panda's head. They should be placed approximately 2¼ inches (5.7 cm) apart from the inside of both ears. Work a running stitch with four strands of white thread around the perimeter of both ears.

3. Embroider around the perimeter of the panda's head using six strands of the dark burnt orange thread.

4. Next, transfer the inner ear templates (#7) onto the black felt. Pin both inner ears into the bottom-center of the white ears. Use a running stitch with three strands of black floss around the perimeter of the inner ears. Save the remaining three strands for the red panda's nose.

5. Transfer the red panda's muzzle template (#2) onto the white felt. Secure the white muzzle to the bottom-center of the panda's head. Use your ruler to make sure it is centered at the bottom of the face. Work a running stitch with four strands of white floss around the border of the muzzle. Reserve the remaining white floss for the cheeks.

6. When the muzzle is embroidered, you are ready to transfer the red panda's cheeks (#3) onto the white felt. Pin the cheeks into position on the sides of the muzzle. The cheeks are approximately ¼ inch (6 mm) from the muzzle on both sides. Use four strands of white thread to embroider a running stitch around the border of each cheek.

7. Transfer the red panda's nose template (#4) onto the black felt and pin it in the center of the white muzzle. Work a running stitch with three strands of black thread around the border. Save any remaining floss for the panda's face embroidery work.

8. For the last transfer step, transfer the panda's eyebrow templates (#5) onto the white felt and set them aside until you embroider the eyes.

(continued)

Embroidery Instructions

1.   First use your fabric pen to draw the red panda's eyes. Use the Red Panda-monium picture in the book for placement references. The eyes are ¾ inch (2 cm) in length from corner to corner. With a backstitch, use three strands of black embroidery floss to stitch the eyes. Add two eyelashes to both eyes using a straight stitch.

2.   When the eyes are embroidered, secure the white felt eyebrows over the inner corners of both eyes. Make a single horizontal straight stitch using two strands of white floss in the center of both eyebrows to secure them in place.

3.   For the red panda's mouth, draw a straight vertical line descending from the tip of the nose. The line should be a little over ⅛ inch (3 mm) in length. At the bottom of the vertical line, draw a horizontal line a little over ¼ inch (6 mm) in length that slightly curves upward at both ends. Use three strands of black thread to embroider the lines of the mouth.

TURTLE-Y CUTE

Some of my happiest memories from childhood are of catching turtles with my dad. This cute turtle pattern is an ode to those memories. The layers of multiple felt pieces give the turtle a really neat multidimensional look that wouldn't be possible using only embroidery floss. Use felts and threads in earth tones as shown, or customize your turtle with colors of your own.

Patterns/Templates: page 125

Stitches: Running stitch (page 19), straight stitch (page 18), backstitch (page 19) and French knot (page 21)

Hoop size: 5-inch (13-cm) round

Fabric: 7-inch (18-cm) square of fabric (ivory)

Felt colors: Olive-green, calico blue, heathered light brown and light brown

Embroidery floss colors: Light antique blue, dark moss green, light drab brown, dark brown and ultra very light terra cotta

Other materials: Fabric scissors, paper scissors, regular adhesive tape, straight pins, embroidery needle, water-soluble fabric pen and ruler

---

Hoop the fabric and trim the excess, leaving at least 1 inch (2.5 cm) excess around the entire hoop.

Template Transfer and Felt Fabric Instructions

1. Transfer the turtle shell template (#1) onto the olive-green felt fabric and secure it to the center of the hoop with straight pins. Before you embroider the shell into place, transfer, position and embroider the feet (#4) onto the hoop.

2. Transfer the foot templates (#4) onto the calico blue felt fabric. Use straight pins to pin the feet onto the fabric approximately 2 inches (5 cm) apart. The top of the feet will just barely meet up with the bottom of the shell; any gap between the two will be covered up by the rim of the shell (#2). Pin the feet into place. Using three strands of the light antique blue floss, embroider a running stitch along the perimeter of each foot.

3. Next, with three strands of the dark moss green floss, use a running stitch to embroider the olive-green shell onto the fabric.

4. When the feet and shell are in place, you are ready to begin transferring and embroidering the shell plates. While you can certainly transfer and embroider the plates all at once, I transferred and pinned my plates into place one at a time in order to achieve my desired placement and look. Please keep in mind, while placing your plates, to leave a border of the exposed olive-green shell underneath each of the plates.

5. Begin by transferring the top plate (#5) onto the heathered light brown felt, and pin it into place at the top of the shell.

6. Transfer the middle row next, starting with the far-left plate (#6). Pin it into place. Transfer and pin the remaining middle row plates (#7 and #8) next.

7. When the middle row is pinned into position, transfer the bottom row of plates next, starting with #9. Keep in mind that the bottom of this last row of plates will line up with the bottom of the turtle shell, which will be partially covered by the rim of the shell (#2). Transfer and pin the remaining three bottom row plates (#10, #11 and #12).

8. Now that all of the plates are pinned in place, you are ready to embroider along the border of each with three strands of the light drab brown floss in a running stitch. As you did with the template transfer, work from the top plate down, removing the pins as you go.

(continued)

9. When the plates are embroidered, transfer the rim of the shell template (#2) onto the light brown felt and pin it into place using one or two straight pins. The rim of the shell should overlap both the bottom of the shell/plates and the top of the feet and cover any gap between the two. Before you embroider the rim of the shell, transfer and stitch the turtle's tail (#13) into place.

10. After you transfer the turtle's tail (#13) onto the calico blue felt, place the tail at the end of the base of the shell on the right-hand side. The tail should slightly tuck under the rim. Stitch it into place with a straight stitch using three strands of light antique blue thread.

11. Now, with three strands of light drab brown embroidery floss, embroider the rim of the shell in a backstitch that runs along the center of the entire length of the rim.

12. The last transfer step is to transfer the turtle's head (#3) onto the calico blue felt. Pin the head into place partially overlapping the shell and plates on the left-hand side of the shell. Work a running stitch with three strands of light antique blue floss around the perimeter of the head.

Embroidery Instructions

1. First use your fabric pen to mark the turtle's eyes, mouth and cheeks. Use the Turtle-y Cute picture on the previous page for placement references. I used my ruler to mark even placement of the face and mouth, leaving approximately ¼ inch (6 mm) of space between the two eyes. To embroider the eyes and mouth, use three strands of dark brown floss to backstitch over your marked lines.

2. To complete the face, embroider a French knot with three strands of ultra very light terra cotta thread on both sides of the mouth.

DON'T BE JEALOUS JELLYFISH

In the sea of life, don't be a jealous jellyfish. This friendly reminder in the form of an embroidered felt jellyfish is easily achieved with just three basic stitches. It's the perfect project for beginners . . . or those prone to jealousy.

Patterns/Templates: page 127

Stitches: Running stitch (page 19), backstitch (page 19) and straight stitch (page 18)

Hoop size: 5-inch (13-cm) round

Fabric: 7-inch (18-cm) square of fabric (light gray with scattered white dots)

Felt colors: Coral and light pink

Embroidery floss colors: Light pink, coral and gray

Other materials: Fabric scissors, paper scissors, regular adhesive tape, straight pins, ruler, embroidery needle and water-soluble fabric pen

Hoop the fabric and trim the excess, leaving at least 1 inch (2.5 cm) excess around the entire hoop.

Template Transfer and Felt Fabric Instructions

1.   Transfer the jellyfish body template (#1) onto the coral felt fabric. Next, secure the coral felt body to the hoop fabric with two straight pins. Wait to embroider the body until the tentacles have been transferred and stitched into place.

2.   Transfer the jellyfish tentacles (#3, #4, #5 and #6) onto the light pink felt fabric. Use a straight pin to secure each tentacle into position on the fabric. The body of the jellyfish should slightly overlap the tops of the tentacles. I started by pinning the two outer tentacles first (#3 and #6) to make it easier to get even placement of all four tentacles. The outer tentacles should be placed approximately ¼ inch (6 mm) in from the outer corners of the body. I placed the center two tentacles next (#4 and #5) about ½ inch (1.3 cm) apart.

3.   To embroider the tentacles, work a running stitch with two strands of light pink embroidery thread down the center of each tentacle.

4.   When the tentacles have been embroidered, use a running stitch, with three strands of coral floss, to embroider along the border of the jellyfish body.

5.   For the last transfer step, transfer the jellyfish's cheeks (#2) onto the light pink felt and set them aside. Reserve the stitching of the cheeks until the remainder of the face has been marked and embroidered.

Embroidery Instructions

1.   First, use your fabric pen to draw the jellyfish's face. I used a ruler to measure out the distance between the eyes (about ½ inch [1.3 cm] apart). The eyes are drawn to look like upside-down curved lines. The mouth should be centered below the two eyes in the shape of a U. Using two strands of gray floss, backstitch in the eyes and mouth.

2.   The final step is to place a straight stitch in the center of each cheek to secure them on either side of the jellyfish's mouth. I eyeballed their placement rather than measuring, but they are about ¼ inch (6 mm) from the mouth on both sides. Use two strands of the coral thread for the straight stitches.

felted feelings AND WHIMSY

The following section of patterns is the heart of my Etsy shop, Olive & Fox. They encompass a variety of feelings and whimsical work that pull straight from my love of books, outdoor adventuring and family. They represent fairy-tale characters, such as the Little Mermaid, that I've loved since I was a child, or interests I now share with my own children, such as exploring the solar system. These finished projects lend themselves particularly well to nurseries and children's rooms with well-loved décor themes including space, adventure and florals.

These are some of the most challenging projects in the book and often require intricate template transfer cuts, multiple stitching techniques and the precise placement and embroidery of multiple felt pieces to achieve the desired results. Take your time layering and pinning the felt pieces into place. Work with small, sharp scissors for challenging cuts, and use a sharp needle to embroider through layers of felt and fabric. With patience and the correct tools, the end result will be a collection of beautiful pieces that make for thoughtful gifts and keepsakes.

HOME IS WHEREVER I'M WITH YOU

Nothing makes me happier or more centered than adventuring with my family, proving that "home" is a feeling we carry in our hearts. This updated version of my beloved Happy Camper hoop conveys that feeling through the text. The charming retro-inspired design lends itself well to bright and colorful felts. And while there are lots of small components to the design, the embroidery work is relatively simple, making this a great gift idea for those who make you feel like "home." For an extra-special touch, use a 6-inch (15-cm) hoop and embroider a family's last name or a special year underneath the text at the bottom of the design!

Patterns/Templates: page 129

Stitches: Backstitch (page 19), running stitch (page 19), straight stitch (page 18) and French knot (page 21)

Hoop size: 5-inch (13-cm) round

Fabric: 7-inch (18-cm) square of fabric (white with polka dots)

Felt colors: White, coral, light yellow, black, peach and turquoise

Embroidery floss colors: Coral, white, dark gray, light gray, light yellow and peach

Other materials: Water-soluble fabric pen, fabric scissors, paper scissors, regular adhesive tape, straight pins and embroidery needle

Pattern Transfer Instructions

1.   Transfer the text pattern onto your fabric.

2.   Hoop the fabric and trim the excess, leaving at least 1 inch (2.5 cm) excess around the entire hoop.

Text Embroidery Instructions

1.   With three strands of the coral embroidery floss, use a backstitch to embroider the letters of the text. To prevent pulling and distortion of the fabric between letters, backstitch each word separately. Knot the floss after the last stitch to prevent unraveling and cut off the excess floss before moving on to stitch the next word.

Felt Template Transfer and Embroidery Instructions

1.   Start by transferring the main camper body template (#1) onto the white felt fabric. After centering the camper body in the middle of the fabric, stitch it into place using a running stitch with two strands of white embroidery floss.

2.   Transfer the lower camper trim template (#2) onto the coral felt fabric. Pin it into position overlapping the bottom of the white camper body. Embroider the camper trim using a running stitch with two strands of coral embroidery floss.

3.   For the camper door, use your fabric pen to make a vertical rectangle that's centered in the middle of the camper body. Embroider over your marks using a backstitch with two strands of dark gray embroidery floss. Make a horizontal straight stitch for a door handle halfway down the door. With the three strands of dark gray floss, make a long horizontal straight stitch off the right bottom edge of the camper to serve as the camper's hitch.

(continued)

4. Next, transfer the three window templates (#3, #4 and #5) onto the light yellow felt. Straight pin the two rectangle windows into place with the larger of the two (#5) being placed on the left-hand side of the door and the smaller (#4) on the right. Use two strands of your light gray floss to make four straight stitches around the perimeter of both windows to mimic metallic window trim. The round window (#3) for the camper door can be held in place while you use two strands of light yellow floss to make one straight stitch in the center of the circle.

5. Transfer the tire template (#6) onto the black felt and pin it onto the bottom left-hand side of the camper. With six strands of the light gray floss, make a French knot in the center of the tire for the hubcap.

6. The last step is to transfer and embroider the decorative triangle banner (#7). Start by transferring the triangles onto the peach and turquoise felt. Transfer three of each color. Lay out the felt triangles running across the top portion of the camper over the door and windows. They are too small to pin; hold them in place with your fingers as you embroider them. Use two strands of peach embroidery floss to backstitch across the tops of the triangles. Your backstitches should meet up in the top center of each triangle which secures them to your camper and fabric.

THE BOY WHO LIVED

The Harry Potter *book series is one of my all-time favorites, and I knew a book of whimsical patterns wouldn't be complete without The Boy Who Lived! Harry is one of the more detailed and challenging designs in this book. The transfer process will take extra care and attention, so give yourself plenty of time. Work with small, sharp scissors to cut the tight angles of his hair and the circles of his glasses. The extra effort will be worth it in the end, and I think you will be quite pleased with how Harry "comes to life" with each piece of carefully placed felt.*

Patterns/Templates: page 131

Stitches: Running stitch (page 19), straight stitch (page 18) and backstitch (page 19)

Hoop size: 7-inch (18-cm) round

Fabric: 9-inch (23-cm) square of fabric (ivory)

Felt colors: Black, burgundy, light peach and yellow-gold

Embroidery floss colors: Black, burgundy, yellow-gold, light desert sand and medium desert sand

Other materials: Fabric scissors, paper scissors, regular adhesive tape, straight pins, embroidery needle and water-soluble fabric pen

Hoop the fabric and trim the excess, leaving at least 1 inch (2.5 cm) excess around the entire hoop.

Template Transfer and Felt Fabric Instructions

1. Transfer Harry's bust (#3) onto the black felt fabric. Next, secure his bust to the hoop fabric with two straight pins. The bottom of the bust should line up with where the inner hoop starts, which means a thin strip of fabric will be visible between the edge of the bust and the outer hoop ring. Use six strands of black embroidery floss to running stitch the bust into place.

2. Transfer the scarf template (#5) onto the burgundy felt. Pin the scarf into place on top of the bust. The end of the scarf tail should meet up with the bottom of the bust. Before you embroider the scarf, transfer the head template (#1) onto the light peach felt to make sure the head and scarf line up properly. Set the head aside while you embroider the scarf with three strands of burgundy thread in a running stitch.

3. Next, transfer the scarf square templates (#6, #7, #8, #9 and #10) onto the yellow-gold felt. Pin them into place in the order you transferred them. Templates #6, #7 and #8 should go on the portion of the scarf wrapped around Harry's neck while #9 and #10 should go on the tail of the scarf. Refer to their placement in The Boy Who Lived photograph, if needed. Using three strands of yellow-gold floss, running stitch around the border of each yellow-gold scarf square.

4. When the scarf is complete, pin Harry's head onto the fabric. The bottom of his face should meet up with the top of the scarf. Work a running stitch with three strands of the light desert sand thread around the perimeter of his face.

5. Transfer his hair (#2) onto the black felt. I recommend using small fabric and paper scissors for this portion of the transfer process due to the tight angles of his hair. Use two straight pins to pin his hair into place on top of his head. Wait to embroider his hair until his glasses are in place.

6. Now transfer his glasses (#4) onto the black felt. This is the trickiest part of the transfer process so take your time. To cut out the center of his glasses, fold the paper template in half over the circle. Use small paper scissors to make a small cut on the fold, then use the point of your scissors to widen the cut until you're able to work your scissors around the inside of the circle. Remove the paper from the inside circle of his glasses, and repeat on the other side of the glasses. Use the same technique for removing the felt from the center of his glasses. As an FYI in case the same happens to you, I accidentally cut a portion of the paper template while removing the paper from the inner circle. It was no big deal since I was able to use a piece of tape to line up the cut pieces properly when I taped the paper template to the felt.

(continued)

7.   Lay his glasses on his face and keep in mind that some of his bangs and hair will overlap his glasses. When you have his glasses in place, use a straight pin or your hand to hold them in place. Work a running stitch along the glasses with two strands of black thread.

8.   When the glasses are embroidered, you can stitch along the border of his hair with three strands of black thread. I used a running stitch for his hair along with a few straight stitches on the sections of his hair that stick out.

9.   The final transfer step is to transfer his badge (#11) onto the yellow-gold felt. Make one or two straight stitches with three strands of yellow-gold floss in the center of the badge to secure it to the right side of his chest.

Embroidery Instructions

1.   Now you are ready to embroider Harry's facial features and scar. Begin by marking his eyes and eyebrows in the center of his glasses with your fabric pen. His eyes are in the shape of upside-down U's and his eyebrows are a straight line over each eye. Use three strands of black embroidery floss to backstitch each eye. The eyebrows are a single straight stitch with the black thread.

2.   Next, mark Harry's nose and mouth with your fabric pen. The nose is drawn with a small curved line, and the mouth is a U shape. Using three strands of the light desert sand floss, backstitch over his nose. Work a backstitch with three strands of the medium desert sand floss for his mouth.

3.   The final step is to give Harry his famous scar. Use your fabric pen to draw a small lightning bolt shape in the opening above the left circle of his glasses. With two strands of the medium desert sand embroidery floss, embroider the scar with a backstitch.

ADVENTURE IS CALLING

My favorite weekends are those spent outdoors, hiking through the woods. Busy schedules often prevent us from doing so, but I always hear the adventure calling. This beautiful piece is a celebration of my love for the outdoors, and it would be delightful in a nature-inspired nursery or kid's room. The design, which is deceptively simple, requires only three types of embroidery stitches. Advanced embroidery lovers might enjoy adding some embroidered flowers at the base of the mountain for a feminine touch.

Patterns/Templates: pages 133 and 135

Stitches: Backstitch (page 19), French knot (page 21) and running stitch (page 19)

Hoop size: 7-inch (18-cm) round

Fabric: 9-inch (23-cm) square of fabric (white)

Felt colors: Light yellow, light gray and white

Embroidery floss colors: Medium antique blue, pale yellow and dark gray

Other materials: Water-soluble fabric pen, fabric scissors, paper scissors, regular adhesive tape, straight pins and embroidery needle

Pattern Transfer Instructions

1. Transfer the Adventure is Calling text pattern onto your fabric.

2. Hoop the fabric, with the text at the top. Trim the excess, leaving at least 1 inch (2.5 cm) excess around the entire hoop.

Text Embroidery Instructions

1. With three strands of medium antique blue thread, use a backstitch to embroider the text. To prevent pulling and distortion of the fabric between words, backstitch each word separately. Knot the floss after the last stitch to prevent unraveling, and cut off the excess floss before moving on to stitch the next word. The ellipsis after "calling" is stitched with a series of three French knots using the three strands of the medium antique blue thread.

Felt Template Transfer and Embroidery Instructions

1. To get the correct placement of the mountains and sun, begin by transferring them both. Transfer the sun template (#1) onto the light yellow felt fabric. The mountains template (#2) should be transferred onto the light gray felt. Lay them out on your hooped fabric with the sun first and the mountains on top. The sun should have the appearance of rising from behind the mountains, but be sure that the sun or mountains do not cover your text. When you have the sun in the correct position, pin it into place with two or three straight pins and set the mountains aside.

2. Stitch the sun into place, with three strands of pale yellow floss, using a running stitch.

3. Now lay the mountains back into place over the sun. Secure them to the fabric with three or four pins. Before you embroider the mountains, transfer and pin the snowy mountain peaks (templates #3, #4 and #5) onto the white felt. Pin each snowy peak at the top of the corresponding mountain: #3 should be pinned on top of the center mountain, #4 on the left mountain and #5 on the right mountain.

4. When the snowy peaks are pinned at the top of each mountain, you are ready to embroider along the perimeter of the mountains and their peaks. Use four strands of the dark gray floss and work a running stitch along the border, including the outer border of the white snowy peaks.

5. After you've completed the mountain borders, embroider a running stitch, with four strands of dark gray thread, along the jagged edges of the white snowy peaks.

6. Lastly, use four strands of dark gray floss to add some details to the mountains. I've done this by backstitching upside-down V's scattered across the light gray mountain felt. There is no rhyme or reason to their placement; rather, I simply stitched them where I found them to be pleasing to the eye.

MAKE A SPLASH MERMAID

As a young girl, I was obsessed with The Little Mermaid *and dreamed of being Ariel. To give my favorite childhood princess a fresh, modern look, I used light brown, mauve and aqua wool-blend felts. While this mermaid was created on a 6-inch (15-cm) scalloped wood hoop from Auburn Hoops, you could increase the hoop size if you'd like to incorporate custom text or name embroidery (page 99) into the design.*

Patterns/Templates: page 137

Stitches: Running stitch (page 19), backstitch (page 19), straight stitch (page 18) and French knot (page 21)

Hoop size: 6-inch (15-cm) round

Fabric: 8-inch (20-cm) square of fabric (aqua blue with wavy line pattern)

Felt colors: Mauve, light brown, mint, aqua and lavender

Embroidery floss colors: Mauve, light beige brown, mint, light sea green, light grape, black, light pink and aqua

Other materials: Fabric scissors, paper scissors, regular adhesive tape, straight pins, embroidery needle, water-soluble fabric pen and ruler

Hoop the fabric and trim the excess, leaving at least 1 inch (2.5 cm) excess around the entire hoop.

Template Transfer and Felt Fabric Instructions

1. For this project, it may be helpful to transfer the mermaid's head (#6), hair (#2), torso with arms (#1), waist (#5) and tail (#4) onto their respective felts first to map out their placement on the hooped fabric. When you have an idea of how the pieces line up together, you can pin and embroider them in the order outlined in the following steps.

2. Transfer the mermaid's hair (#2) and bangs (#3) onto the mauve felt fabric. Reserve the bangs for after you stitch the mermaid's head. Work three strands of mauve floss in a running stitch along the perimeter of her hair.

3. Transfer the torso/arms template (#1) onto the light brown felt. Use straight pins to secure the torso to the center of the hooped fabric. The neck, shoulders and upper arms will overlap some of the hair (refer to the picture). With two strands of light beige brown embroidery thread, work a running stitch along the border of the torso and arms.

4. Transfer the mermaid's head (#6) onto the light brown felt. Pin the head at the top of the neck, and embroider around the perimeter with two strands of light beige brown thread.

5. When the head is in place, pin the bangs (#3) into position at the top of the mermaid's head. Embroider a running stitch along the border of the bangs with two strands of mauve floss.

6. Transfer the mermaid's tail (#4) onto the mint felt and the waist template (#5) onto the aqua felt. Line the tail up with the torso and pin it into place. Set aside the waist until the tail has been stitched. Use three strands of mint thread to embroider a running stitch along the perimeter of the tail.

7. The waist (#5) will overlap both the torso and the tail. Pin the waist into place and, using three strands of light sea green floss, embroider two straight stitches along the waist that meet in the center of the waist where the V forms.

8. Transfer the mermaid's top (#7) onto the lavender felt and pin it onto the torso. Use two strands of light grape thread to stitch a running stitch along the border of the top.

Embroidery Instructions

1. Start by drawing the mermaid's facial features with your fabric pen. Use a ruler to mark your preferred eye, nose, mouth and cheek placement. The eyes are drawn with a curved line with two lashes at each outer corner. Embroider the lines with two strands of black thread in a backstitch. Use two small straight stitches on each eye for the lashes.

2. The nose is a small upwards curved line that should be embroidered with a backstitch using two strands of the light beige brown floss. For the mouth, draw a U shape and embroider with two strands of mauve floss using a backstitch.

3. When you've embroidered the mouth, use six strands of the light pink thread to embroider a French knot for each cheek.

4. For the mermaid's tail fins, mark one line in the center of each fin. Embroider a single ½ inch (1.3 cm) straight stitch, with three strands of the aqua floss, over the marked lines.

DINO-ROAR

This dinosaur is ready to greet all who enter your home with a friendly ROAR! Transferring the dinosaur template is the trickiest part of the design with only a running stitch and backstitch required for the embroidery work. For the template transfer portion, be sure to have small fabric scissors to cut into tight spaces around the dinosaur's legs and use plenty of tape to secure the body to the felt. With a steady hand and a bit of patience, you'll bring this dinosaur to life in no time!

Patterns/Templates: page 139

Stitches: Running stitch (page 19) and backstitch (page 19)

Hoop size: 7-inch (18-cm) round

Fabric: 9-inch (23-cm) square of fabric (light yellow)

Felt colors: Mint and dark green

Embroidery floss colors: Mint, dark fern green and black

Other materials: Fabric scissors, paper scissors, regular adhesive tape, straight pins, embroidery needle and water-soluble fabric pen

Hoop the fabric and trim the excess, leaving at least 1 inch (2.5 cm) excess around the entire hoop.

Template Transfer and Felt Fabric Instructions

1. Transfer the dinosaur template (#1) onto the mint felt fabric. Next, secure the mint felt body to the hoop fabric with three or four straight pins. Stitch the dinosaur body into place, with three strands of the mint embroidery floss, using a running stitch.

2. Transfer the dinosaur scale templates (#2 through #7) onto the dark green felt fabric. Transfer one scale at a time, starting with #2 at the top and working your way down the dinosaur's back and tail. Pin each scale into place before transferring the next scale, which will help you to lay the scales in the correct order on the dinosaur's back. Use two strands of the dark fern green embroidery floss to secure each scale into place with a running stitch.

Embroidery Instructions

1. For the dinosaur's face, use two strands of black embroidery floss to backstitch the eye (an upside-down U shape) and mouth.

2. To complete the dinosaur's legs, use two strands of mint embroidery floss to backstitch the dashed lines (A and B) that are shown on the dinosaur template (#1).

Text Embroidery Instructions

1. Remove the fabric from the hoop to transfer the ROAR text and word bubble pattern onto your fabric. The tip of the word bubble should look like it's coming out of the dinosaur's mouth. Use the Dino-Roar picture on the next page for a placement reference. Re-hoop the fabric. When the text and word bubble are transferred and the fabric is back on the hoop, use two strands of the black embroidery floss to backstitch the letters and outline of the word bubble on the fabric.

YOU ARE LOVED

You are loved is one of my favorite expressions for a baby's nursery, and I designed this pattern with that in mind. The project uses soft, feminine colors to make a pretty statement. The satin stitched florals are especially charming and make for a beautiful keepsake for new parents. For a more gender-neutral piece, simply use different colored fabric, floss or felt, and omit the floral portion of the design. Here I used a 7-inch (18-cm) round specialty hoop from Auburn Hoops.

Patterns/Templates: page 141

Stitches: Backstitch (page 19), satin stitch (page 20), detached chain stitch (page 21) and French knot (page 21)

Hoop size: 7-inch (18-cm) round

Fabric: 9-inch (23-cm) square of fabric (blush with scattered white dots)

Felt colors: Mustard yellow

Embroidery floss colors: Light terra cotta, dark old gold, medium desert sand, ultra very light terra cotta, very light desert sand and fern green

Other materials: Water-soluble fabric pen, fabric scissors, paper scissors, regular adhesive tape, straight pins and embroidery needle

Pattern Transfer Instructions

1. Transfer the You Are Loved text pattern and floral design onto your fabric. "You Are" is a felt template; however, for correct placement of the felt letters, you can transfer the "You Are" text to the fabric to guide you as you place and embroider the felt letters.

2. Hoop the fabric, with the text centered and the floral design centered at the bottom of the hoop. Trim the excess, leaving at least 1 inch (2.5 cm) excess around the entire hoop.

Text Embroidery Instructions

1. With six strands of light terra cotta, use a backstitch to embroider the word "Loved." For the portions of the letters that are thicker, use additional backstitches to fill them in. Offset the additional backstitches from the original line of backstitches.

Embroidery Instructions

1. Begin by embroidering the center flower first. Use a horizontal satin stitch, with three strands of dark old gold floss, to fill the center of the flower. When the center is complete, work in a clockwise motion to satin stitch the petals with three strands of the light terra cotta thread.

2. Embroider the outer flowers next using a satin stitch. Stitch the center of each flower first with a horizontal satin stitch using three strands of medium desert sand floss. Work a vertical satin stitch in a clockwise motion, with three strands of ultra very light terra cotta thread, around the middle portion of both outer flowers. For the outer layer of both flowers, embroider a vertical satin stitch using three strands of very light desert sand thread.

3. For the vines, work a backstitch with three strands of fern green thread over the vine pattern. When that's complete, you can embroider the leaves. Starting on the left vine, use a detached chain stitch on both sides of the vine to embroider the leaf pattern. Repeat on the right side of the hoop.

4. At the top of each vine, embroider three French knots in a triangle pattern using six strands of the medium desert sand floss.

Felt Template Transfer and Embroidery Instructions

1. Transfer the You Are template onto the mustard yellow felt. The letters should be centered in an arc above the word Loved. If you transferred "You Are" during the pattern transfer process, you can pin and embroider your felt letters directly over your transferred lines. Work a backstitch, with two strands of ultra very light terra cotta thread, along the center of each letter to secure them to the fabric. Refer to the photograph of the finished You Are Loved project, if needed.

OH, THE PLACES YOU'LL GO

It's always been my dream to own a vintage Volkswagen Beetle in a snazzy color . . . oh, the places I'd go! With nine felt templates, this is one of the most intricate designs in the book, but I'll walk you through every step. Before you know it, you'll have your very own retro car with dreams of epic road trips!

Patterns/Templates: page 143

Stitches: Backstitch (page 19), running stitch (page 19) and straight stitch (page 18)

Hoop size: 7-inch (18-cm) round

Fabric: 8-inch (20-cm) square of fabric (white)

Felt colors: Peacock, light gray and black

Embroidery floss colors: Black, dark peacock blue, light gray, dark gray and very dark peacock blue

Other materials: Water-soluble fabric pen, fabric scissors, embroidery needle, paper scissors, regular adhesive tape, straight pins and ruler

Pattern Transfer Instructions

1. Transfer the text pattern onto your fabric.

2. Hoop the fabric, with the text centered towards the bottom. Trim the excess, leaving at least 1 inch (2.5 cm) excess around the entire hoop.

Text Embroidery Instructions

1. With two strands of the black embroidery floss, use a backstitch to embroider the text. To prevent the black thread from being seen against the fabric, knot and cut off the excess thread between each word.

Felt Template Transfer and Embroidery Instructions

1. Start by transferring the car body template (#1) onto the peacock felt and the car exhaust template (#9) onto the light gray felt. Use straight pins to secure the car and exhaust to the fabric centered above the text. Refer to the Oh, the Places You'll Go picture for placement purposes. Remember to leave space for the tires so they don't overlap the text. Work a running stitch with three strands of dark peacock blue embroidery thread around the border of the car.

The car exhaust should be embroidered around the perimeter with three strands of light gray floss in a running stitch.

2. Transfer the tire templates (#3) onto the black felt fabric. Secure both tires to the fabric with pins. The tires should not overlap the car body. Stitch both into place with three strands of black thread in a running stitch.

3. Transfer the hubcaps (#4) onto the light gray felt. Pin a hubcap in the center of both tires, and embroider the perimeter of each with three strands of light gray floss in a running stitch.

4. Transfer the fender templates (#5 and #6) onto the peacock felt. Pin #5 above the front tire and #6 above the rear tire. Embroider both along the perimeter using three strands of dark peacock blue thread in a running stitch.

5. Transfer the window templates (#7 and #8) onto the light gray felt fabric. Secure #7 in the front window position and #8 in the rear window position. There should be a strip of peacock felt visible between the two windows. Work a running stitch with three strands of dark gray thread along the border of both windows.

6. Transfer the door handle template (#2) onto the peacock felt. Place the handle under the right corner of the front window and secure with a single straight stitch using three strands of dark peacock blue floss.

Embroidery Instructions

1. For your reference, I have labeled the additional embroidery steps (A and B) on the car body template (#1) using dashed lines. Use your fabric pen with a ruler to mark line A on the car body. Note that line A does not extend down into the front fender. Embroider a backstitch with three strands of very dark peacock blue thread along line A.

2. With your ruler and pen, mark line B on the car body. Use three strands of very dark peacock blue thread to backstitch over line B.

SPACED OUT

This pattern was inspired by my son, who helped me rediscover my fascination with space. Future astronauts or my fellow space enthusiasts will love this far-out pattern! Use the provided pattern to embroider the planets in their orbits around the sun. Work with the felt and floss colors I've noted below or choose your favorites for your very own embroidered version of the solar system!

Patterns/Templates: page 145

Stitches: Backstitch (page 19), running stitch (page 19) and straight stitch (page 18)

Hoop size: 7-inch (18-cm) round

Fabric: 9-inch (23-cm) square of fabric (white)

Felt colors: Yellow, light grayish-brown, light yellow, calico blue, cinnamon, ginger, ochre, light blue and sky blue

Embroidery floss colors: Black, dark red copper, light topaz, light drab brown, very light topaz, light antique blue, white, dark topaz, light golden brown, medium yellow, light gray and very light antique blue

Other materials: Water-soluble fabric pen, fabric scissors, embroidery needle, paper scissors, regular adhesive tape and straight pins

Pattern Transfer Instructions

1. Transfer the solar system pattern, including the "Spaced Out" text onto your fabric. When transferring the pattern with your fabric pen, be sure to transfer the initials of the planets too, as they indicate where you should place each of the felt planets.

2. Hoop the fabric, with the text offset to the right. Trim the excess, leaving at least 1 inch (2.5 cm) excess around the entire hoop.

Pattern Embroidery Instructions

1. With two strands of black embroidery thread, use a backstitch to embroider the solar system. Do not embroider the initials of the planets or sun as you will place the felt pieces over the initials.

2. To embroider "Spaced Out," switch to two strands of dark red copper thread and backstitch the letters.

Felt Template Transfer and Embroidery Instructions

1. For the sun and each of the planets, you will be working with two strands of the corresponding floss color in a running stitch around the perimeter of the sun/planet unless noted.

2. Begin by transferring the sun template onto the yellow felt. Secure it to the center of the hooped fabric where it's marked on your pattern. Embroider it with the light topaz thread.

3. Transfer Mercury (ME) onto the light grayish-brown felt. It may be too small to pin to the fabric, so use your hand to hold it in place while you embroider a single straight stitch with the light drab brown thread in the center of the planet.

4. Transfer Venus (VE) onto the light yellow felt. Embroider it with the very light topaz floss.

5. Transfer Earth (EA) onto the calico blue felt. After you work a running stitch around the perimeter of Earth with the light antique blue floss, use two strands of white thread to straight stitch some scattered clouds on the planet.

6. Next, transfer Mars (MA) onto the cinnamon-colored felt. Embroider it with the dark topaz floss.

7. Transfer Jupiter (JU) onto the ginger-colored felt. After you embroider a running stitch around the perimeter of Jupiter with the light golden brown thread, use two strands of white thread to backstitch horizontal bands across the planet.

8. Transfer Saturn (SA) onto the ochre felt, and embroider it with the medium yellow floss. Work a row of backstitch, using six strands of light gray thread, around Saturn to give the appearance of its rings.

9. Transfer Uranus (UR) onto the light blue felt, and embroider it with the very light antique blue floss.

10. Lastly, transfer Neptune (NE) onto the sky blue felt, and stitch it with the light antique blue thread.

donut worry
eat sprinkles

Pizza my HEART!

Taco to me

Don't get it twisted.

Love You a Latte!

Ice Scream, You Scream!

felting for FOODIES

I like food puns about as much as I like tacos—which is to say, A LOT! This collection of food-inspired felt embroidery patterns features some of my favorite foods and food puns. Most of these patterns feature simple designs that require only basic stitching techniques; they rely on the colorful, layered felt to do the work. Several of these projects—Taco to Me (page 76), Don't Get It Twisted Pretzel (page 75) and Ice Scream, You Scream (page 79)—pair perfectly together in a fun display. Of course, each of the projects in this chapter would make a sweet gift for a fellow foodie. Just think of it this way: all of the fun with none of the calories or cooking mess.

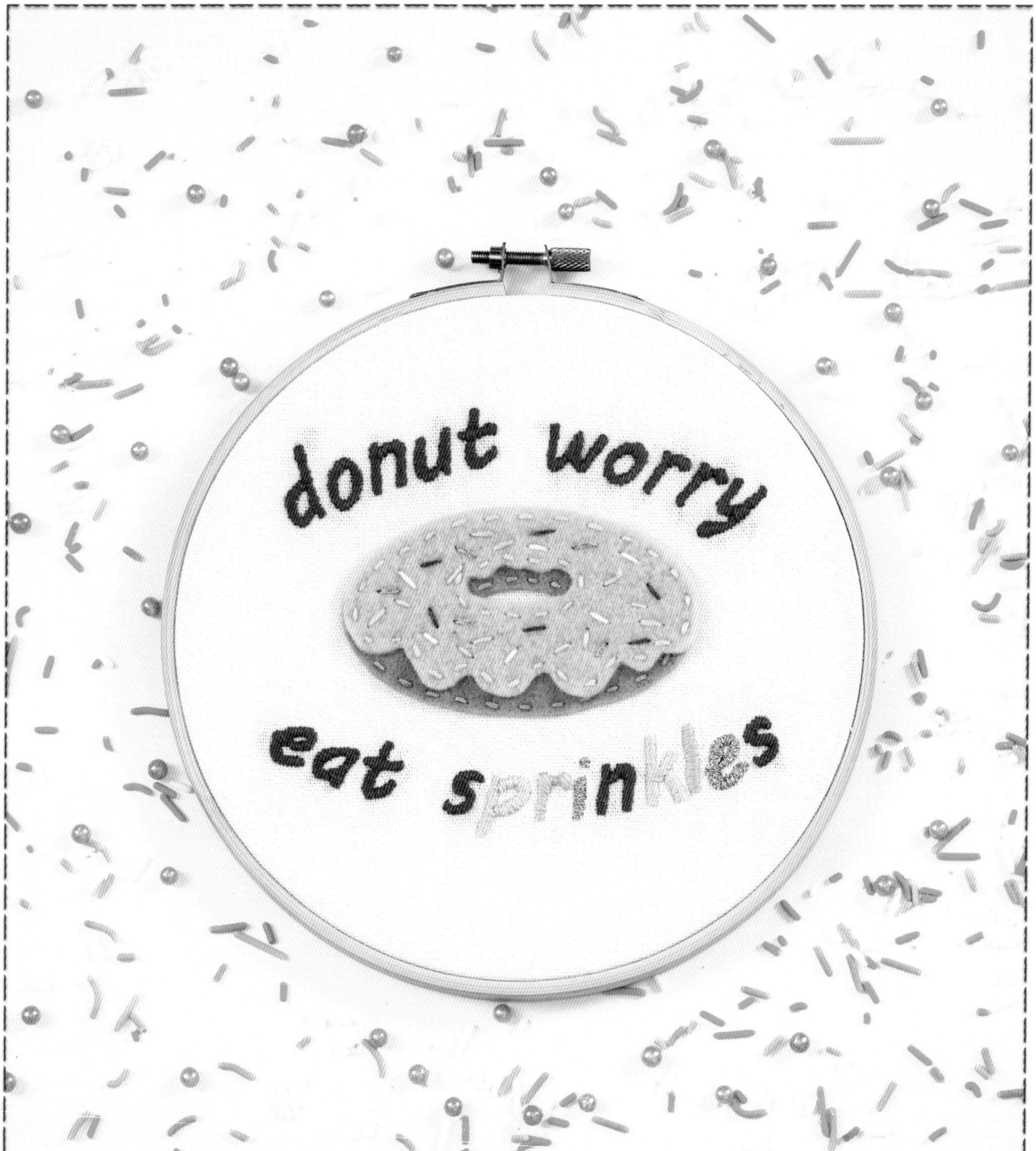
donut worry
eat sprinkles

DONUT WORRY

The Donut Worry pattern is a fresh take on my beloved Donut Worry banner. This updated version uses a satin stitch to give the text a multidimensional look that really pops against the fabric! It's a friendly and delicious reminder not to take daily worries too seriously. After all, there's always donuts . . . extra sprinkles please.

Patterns/Templates: page 147

Stitches: Satin stitch (page 20), running stitch (page 19) and straight stitch (page 18)

Hoop size: 7-inch (18-cm) round

Fabric: 9-inch (23-cm) square of fabric (white)

Felt colors: Tan and light pink

Embroidery floss colors: Dark pink, light pink, light aqua, metallic gold, tan and white

Other materials: Water-soluble fabric pen, fabric scissors, embroidery needle, paper scissors, regular adhesive tape and straight pins

Pattern Transfer Instructions

1. Transfer the Donut Worry and Eat Sprinkles text patterns onto your fabric. "Donut Worry" should be centered at the top of the hooped fabric with "Eat Sprinkles" centered at the bottom of the hooped fabric. Remember to leave space, approximately 3 inches (8 cm), in between the two text patterns for the felt donut.

2. Hoop the fabric and trim the excess, leaving at least 1 inch (2.5 cm) excess around the entire hoop.

Text Embroidery Instructions

1. With four strands of dark pink floss, use a satin stitch to fill in the letters of the text. To prevent pulling and distortion of the fabric between letters, satin stitch each letter separately. Knot the floss after the last stitch to prevent unraveling, and cut off the excess floss before moving on to stitch the next letter. For the word sprinkles, each letter will be embroidered in a different thread color: The n and both s's are dark pink; the p and k are light pink; the r and l are light aqua; the i and e are metallic gold.

Felt Template Transfer and Embroidery Instructions

1. Start by taping the donut template (#1) onto the tan felt fabric. For the inside of the donut hole, use your fabric pen rather than tape to lightly trace around the hole. With your fabric scissors, first cut along the taped template. Next, cut along your marked lines to remove the center of the donut. Secure the tan donut to the hoop fabric using straight pins.

2. Stitch the donut into place, with six strands of tan embroidery floss, using a running stitch. Remove the pins.

3. Transfer the frosting template (#2) onto the light pink felt fabric. Rather than taping along the scalloped frosting at the bottom of the template and the center hole, use your fabric pen to lightly mark these lines on the felt. Cut along the taped template first and then cut along the pen marks of the scalloped frosting edge. Finish by cutting out the center hole of the frosting along your marked lines. Use straight pins to pin the frosting into place on the tan donut.

4. Next, with six strands of light pink embroidery floss, use a running stitch to secure the frosting into place on top of the donut. Remove the pins.

5. For the sprinkles, you can mark their placement with your fabric pen or do it by eye as you stitch along. Use a straight stitch, with six strands of floss, to create the sprinkles with approximately five to seven sprinkles per color of embroidery floss (light pink, dark pink, light aqua, metallic gold and white).

PIZZA MY HEART

This design is dedicated to pizza, which will always and forever be one of my great true loves. I'm not picky when it comes to pizza, but there's definitely beauty to a simple slice of pepperoni. The pattern calls for a satin stitch to fill in the text, which is almost as satisfying to embroider as a slice of pizza pie is to eat! And just like real pizza, this design is versatile. Adventurous embroidery lovers and eaters might enjoy embroidering some additional or different toppings onto their felt pizza slice. Enjoy!

Patterns/Templates: page 149

Stitches: Satin stitch (page 20), running stitch (page 19) and straight stitch (page 18)

Hoop size: 6-inch (15-cm) round

Fabric: 8-inch (20-cm) square of fabric (white)

Felt colors: Antique white, tan, red and ruby

Embroidery floss colors: Medium garnet, tan, ecru, red and medium green

Other materials: Water-soluble fabric pen, fabric scissors, embroidery needle, paper scissors, regular adhesive tape and straight pins

Pattern Transfer Instructions

1. Transfer the Pizza My Heart text pattern onto your fabric.

2. Hoop the fabric, with the text offset to the right. Trim the excess, leaving at least 1 inch (2.5 cm) excess around the entire hoop.

Text Embroidery Instructions

1. With three strands of the medium garnet embroidery floss, work a satin stitch to fill in the letters of the text. You'll be using rows of satin stitch to fill in the text; be sure to offset each row of satin stitches in a brick-like pattern. To prevent pulling and distortion of the fabric between letters, satin stitch each letter separately. Knot the floss after the last stitch to prevent unraveling, and cut off the excess floss before moving on to stitch the next letter.

Felt Template Transfer and Embroidery Instructions

1. Start by transferring the pizza cheese template (#3) onto the antique white felt fabric. Secure the cheese to the hoop fabric using a straight pin.

2. Transfer the crust template (#1) onto the tan felt fabric. Use straight pins to pin the crust into place. The crust and cheese felt pieces should meet up but not overlap each other. Use a running stitch, with three strands of tan embroidery floss, to secure the crust into place. Embroider the cheese into place using a running stitch with three strands of the ecru embroidery floss.

3. Next, transfer the pizza sauce (#2) onto the red felt. Round any sharp edges of felt with your scissors after you remove the tape. Secure the pizza sauce with a straight pin on top of the cheese and crust where the two pieces meet. Use your fingers to guide the edges of the pizza sauce into a curve that mimics the lines of the crust. Work a single row of the running stitch down the center of the sauce with two strands of red thread.

4. Transfer one of the circle-shaped pepperoni templates (#4) and the heart-shaped pepperoni (#5) onto the ruby felt fabric. An extra circle template is provided if needed as circles can be tricky to cut. To cut a circle, hold the scissors steady while moving the template or felt as you cut. Place the pepperoni on top of your cheese as shown in the picture or in your own preferred pattern. Use a scattered straight stitch, with two or three strands of the ecru embroidery floss, to secure each pepperoni into place. For the green herbs, you can mark their placement with your fabric pen or do it by eye as you stitch along. Use three or four satin stitches, with three strands of the medium green embroidery floss, to create each of the green herbs.

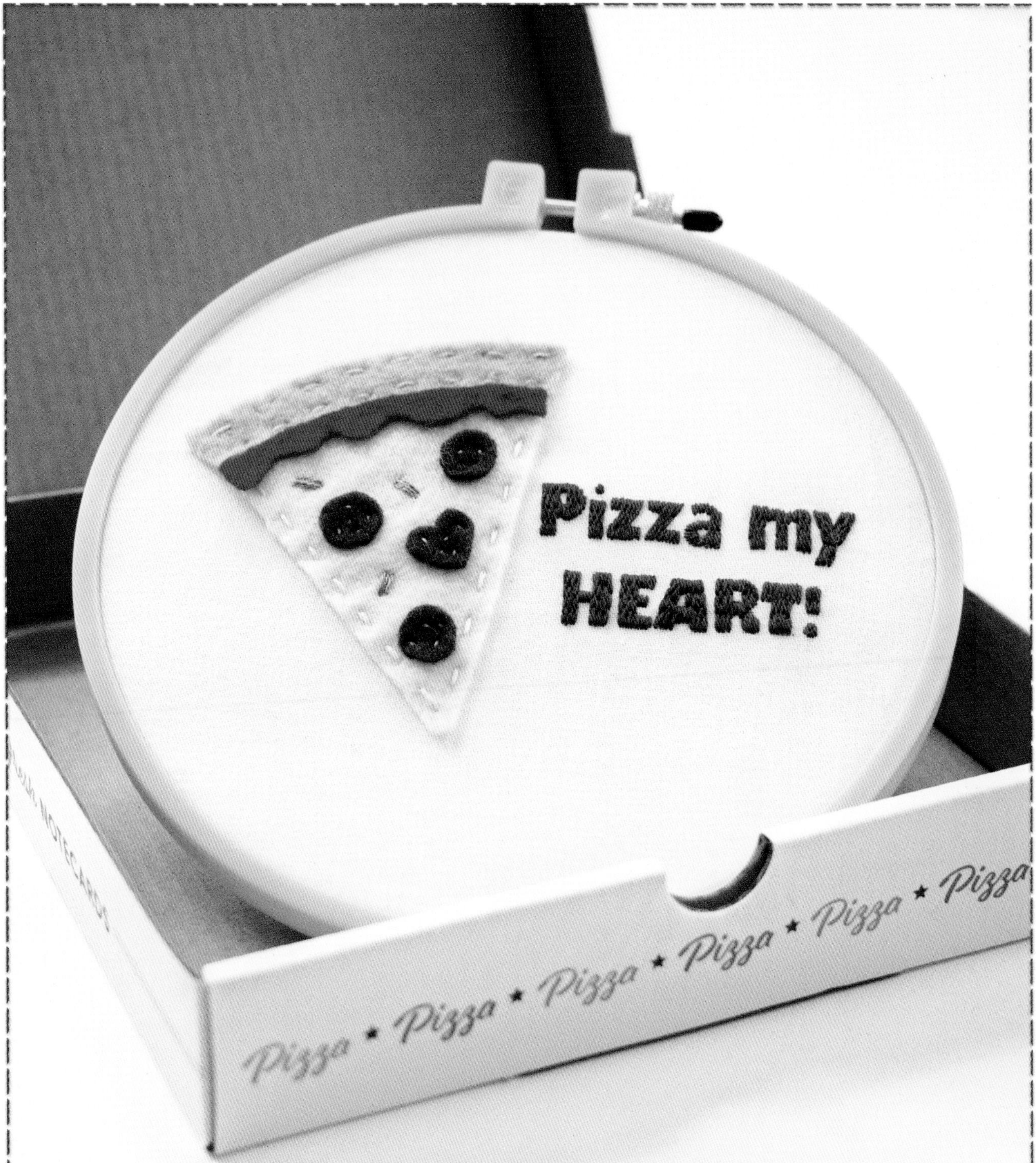
Pizza my
HEART!
Pizza ★ Pizza ★ Pizza ★ Pizza ★ Pizza ★ Pizza

Don't get it twisted.

DON'T GET IT TWISTED PRETZEL

There's nothing like eating an oven-fresh soft pretzel—pulling apart the twist to enjoy every bite. Pretzels are a fun food to eat, so why not have a little pretzel embroidery fun?! Use the provided text pattern, or create your own to accompany the felt pretzel appliqué. The most challenging aspect of this pattern is cutting out the pretzel template, but I've provided some helpful tips so you don't get it twisted. Now for the real dilemma: with or without cheese sauce?

Patterns/Templates: page 151

Stitches: Backstitch (page 19), running stitch (page 19) and straight stitch (page 18)

Hoop size: 5-inch (13-cm) round

Fabric: 7-inch (18-cm) square of fabric (white)

Felt colors: Cinnamon

Embroidery floss colors: Black, light brown, dark brown and white

Other materials: Water-soluble fabric pen, fabric scissors, embroidery needle, paper scissors, regular adhesive tape and straight pins

Pattern Transfer Instructions

1. Transfer the Don't Get it Twisted text pattern onto your fabric.

2. Hoop the fabric, with the text centered towards the bottom. Trim the excess, leaving at least 1 inch (2.5 cm) excess around the entire hoop.

Text Embroidery Instructions

1. With two strands of the black embroidery floss, use a backstitch to embroider the text. To prevent the black thread from being seen against the white fabric, knot and cut off the excess thread between each word.

Felt Template Transfer and Embroidery Instructions

1. Start by transferring the pretzel template onto the cinnamon-colored felt fabric. To remove the excess paper from the center of the pretzel template, fold the template in half where the excess paper at the center of the pretzel is located. Now make a small cut in the center of the fold with your paper scissors while being careful not to cut the template itself. Use the hole to work your scissors into the opening to remove the excess paper from the center. Repeat on the other side of the pretzel and in the small opening under the pretzel twist. You will need to use the same technique with your fabric scissors when you transfer the template to the felt in order to remove the excess felt from the center of the pretzel.

2. Before I pinned the felt pretzel onto the fabric, I marked the lines of the inner pretzel twist with my fabric pen. Refer to the dashed lines (A through G) on the pretzel template for the line placement. Mark lines A, B, C and D first with your pen. Next, draw lines E and G. The last line to mark is F which runs at a slight curve in the center of the twist.

3. When the embroidery lines are marked, secure the pretzel to the hoop fabric using two or three straight pins. Use three strands of the light brown floss to work a running stitch around the outside border of the pretzel, including the outside border at the center of the pretzel. Next, embroider a running stitch along the inside border of the pretzel.

4. Now that the borders have been stitched, use three strands of dark brown thread to backstitch along the embroidery lines you marked with your fabric pen. I embroidered mine in the same order I marked them.

5. The final step is to straight stitch the "salt" with six strands of white floss in a scattered pattern across the pretzel.

TACO TO ME

Tacos shouldn't be reserved solely for Tuesdays. If you're with me, then this is the project for you! Layer multiple pieces of felt to create an adorably delicious taco that will leave you craving the real deal. Now every day can be taco day at your house.

Patterns/Templates: page 153

Stitches: Backstitch (page 19), running stitch (page 19) and straight stitch (page 18)

Hoop size: 5-inch (13-cm) round

Fabric: 7-inch (18-cm) square of fabric (white)

Felt colors: Light tan, brown, green, yellow-gold and red

Embroidery floss colors: Black, tan, dark brown, green, medium yellow, red and pale yellow

Other materials: Water-soluble fabric pen, fabric scissors, embroidery needle, paper scissors, regular adhesive tape and straight pins

Pattern Transfer Instructions

1. Transfer the Taco to Me text pattern onto your fabric.

2. Hoop the fabric, with the text centered towards the bottom. Trim the excess, leaving at least 1 inch (2.5 cm) excess around the entire hoop.

Text Embroidery Instructions

1. With two strands of the black embroidery floss, use a backstitch to embroider the text. To prevent the black thread from being seen against the white fabric, knot and cut off the excess thread between each word.

Felt Template Transfer and Embroidery Instructions

1. Start by transferring the taco shell template (#1) onto the light tan felt fabric. Secure the shell to the fabric centered above the text with a straight pin. Factor the taco meat and condiments into the design when centering the shell over the text. With three strands of tan embroidery floss, work a running stitch along the border of the shell.

2. Transfer the taco meat template (#2) onto the brown felt. Pin the meat into place on the bottom right side of the taco shell. The curve of the brown felt should line up with the curve of the tan shell felt. Use two strands of dark brown embroidery thread to stitch a running stitch along the border of the brown felt.

3. Now transfer the lettuce template (#3) onto the green felt. The small angles and curves of the lettuce and cheese template may be challenging to cut. Work with sharp, small scissors, and don't overly worry about cutting it precisely to the template. Pin the green lettuce above the brown taco meat. The lettuce will overlap the shell and meat some. With two strands of green thread, work a running stitch around the border of the lettuce.

4. Transfer the cheese template (#4) next onto the yellow-gold felt, and secure it above the lettuce. The cheese follows the curve of the shell and will somewhat overlap the shell. Embroider the perimeter of the cheese with two strands of medium yellow floss in a running stitch.

5. The final transfer step is to transfer the tomato templates (#5) onto the red felt. I included seven squares/rectangles for the tomatoes, but feel free to transfer more or less for your design. I laid my felt tomato pieces out in several different designs before I settled on the design shown in the picture. The tomato pieces are small, and I did not pin them in place. Rather, I relied on the felt fibers to hold them to the fabric while I embroidered a straight stitch with two strands of red thread in each one.

6. I added some additional embroidery details to both the cheese and taco shell to give the taco more texture. To add flecks of dark brown "grain" to the shell, embroider a scattered straight stitch with two strands of dark brown thread across the shell. For the cheese, I used six strands of pale yellow floss to straight stitch "pieces" of cheese. In addition, I "added" extra cheese on the left side of the tomatoes. I did so by making three straight stitches with the six strands of pale yellow floss.

ICE SCREAM, YOU SCREAM

Ice scream, you scream, we all scream for ice cream! Celebrate your love for ice cream with this quirky pattern. Use different colored felts and embroidery floss to create your perfect scoop!

Patterns/Templates: page 155

Stitches: Backstitch (page 19), running stitch (page 19), straight stitch (page 18) and satin stitch (page 20)

Hoop size: 5-inch (13-cm) round

Fabric: 7-inch (18-cm) square of fabric (white)

Felt colors: Tan, light pink, cream and mint

Embroidery floss colors: Black, tan, light pink, ecru, mint and dark brown

Other materials: Water-soluble fabric pen, fabric scissors, embroidery needle, paper scissors, regular adhesive tape, straight pins and ruler

Pattern Transfer Instructions

1. Transfer the Ice Scream, You Scream text pattern onto your fabric.

2. Hoop the fabric, with the text centered towards the bottom. Trim the excess, leaving at least 1 inch (2.5 cm) excess around the entire hoop.

Text Embroidery Instructions

1. With two strands of the black embroidery floss, use a backstitch to embroider the text. To prevent the black thread from being seen against the white fabric, knot and cut off the excess thread between each word.

Felt Template Transfer and Embroidery Instructions

1. Start by transferring each cone template (#1) onto the tan felt fabric. Secure both cones to the fabric using straight pins. The cones should be centered above the words. Be sure to save room above the cones for the ice cream felt pieces. Work a running stitch, using three strands of tan embroidery floss around the perimeter of both cones.

2. Transfer the strawberry ice cream scoop template (#2) onto the light pink felt. Pin the scoop into place above the cone on the left. The bottom of the scoop will overlap the top of the cone. Use three strands of light pink thread to embroider a running stitch around the border of the strawberry scoop.

3. Next, transfer the vanilla scoop template (#3) onto the cream felt, and transfer the mint chocolate chip scoop (#4) onto the mint felt fabric. Secure the vanilla scoop onto the top of the right cone. With three strands of your ecru thread, embroider a running stitch around the border of the vanilla scoop.

4. Pin the mint scoop above the vanilla scoop with the mint slightly overlapping the vanilla scoop. Use three strands of the mint floss to stitch a running stitch around the perimeter of the mint scoop.

5. Now you are ready to embroider the cones' faces and arms. With your fabric pen, draw the eyes and mouth on both cones. For the strawberry cone, I added two lashes at the outer corner of both eyes. Because I wanted the ice cream cones to look as if they could be screaming, I drew their mouths in the shape of a filled-in upside-down U. Embroider their eyes using two strands of black thread in a backstitch. Use a straight stitch for any eyelashes. The mouths should be filled in with two strands of black thread in a satin stitch.

6. Next, use your fabric pen to draw their stick arms. I used my ruler to mark ½-inch (1.3-cm) lines for their arms. Work a backstitch, with two strands of black thread, over your lines. Use three straight stitches per arm for their fingers.

7. The final step is to add the "chocolate chips" to the mint scoop. Do so by using all six strands of dark brown floss to make random straight stitches across the scoop.

LOVE YOU A LATTE

Oh, sweet coffee, how I love thee! Especially when you're served with delightful latte art decorating your foam! With only two basic stitches, this is a quick pattern to stitch up. Naturally, it's best enjoyed while sipping a cup or two of coffee!

Patterns/Templates: page 157

Stitches: Backstitch (page 19) and running stitch (page 19)

Hoop size: 6-inch (15-cm) round

Fabric: 8-inch (20-cm) square of fabric (white with navy blue +'s)

Felt colors: Greenish-blue, light brown and white

Embroidery floss colors: Black, medium jade green, light beige brown and white

Other materials: Water-soluble fabric pen, fabric scissors, embroidery needle, paper scissors, regular adhesive tape and straight pins

Pattern Transfer Instructions

1.   Transfer the Love You a Latte text pattern onto your fabric with the text centered at the bottom of the hooped fabric.

2.   Hoop the fabric and trim the excess, leaving at least 1 inch (2.5 cm) excess around the entire hoop.

Text Embroidery Instructions

1.   With two strands of black embroidery thread, use a backstitch to embroider the text.

Felt Template Transfer and Embroidery Instructions

1.   Start by transferring the plate template (#1) onto the greenish-blue felt. Secure the plate into place centered above the text with straight pins. Work a running stitch with three strands of medium jade green thread around the perimeter of the plate.

2.   Next, transfer the coffee cup template (#2) onto the greenish-blue felt, and pin it into position on top of the plate. Use a running stitch with the medium jade green thread to embroider along the border of the cup and handle. Remember to embroider along the inside border of the handle, too.

3.   Transfer the coffee (#3) onto the light brown felt. Secure it to the top of the coffee cup, leaving a thin border of the greenish-blue cup exposed above the light brown coffee. Work a running stitch with two strands of light beige brown floss around the border of the coffee.

4.   To add the latte art, transfer template #4 onto the white felt. Use two straight pins to secure it to the bottom of the coffee. Use a single row of running stitches with two strands of white floss to embroider across the center of the shape. Reserve the two strands of white floss for the next two transfer/embroidery steps.

5.   Transfer the larger heart (#5) onto the white felt. Pin the heart inside the center of the circular shape with the bottom of the heart overlapping the circular shape. Embroider with two strands of white floss in a running stitch.

6.   Transfer the smaller heart template (#6) onto the white felt. Secure it to the fabric with the tip of the smaller heart just touching the larger heart. Work a running stitch with two strands of white floss around the border of the heart.

flora and FELT

My passion for plants is a relatively newfound one after recently discovering that they're a lovely antidote to the long Minnesota winters. Indeed, the longer and colder the winter, the more houseplants I acquire. Naturally, I had to translate my love of plants into a dedicated chapter of flora-inspired designs! Whether you have a green thumb, black thumb or a color in between like mine, these designs are a fun and simple way to add a bit of green into your home.

Plant-inspired designs are popular in embroidery work, but as you create these projects, observe how felt gives added life to these well-loved embroidery subjects. Some of my favorite patterns in the book, Monstera Madness (page 86), Pot of Pilea (page 90) and Mushroom to Grow (page 89), are prime examples of this effect.

The hoops in this section look best when displayed in duos or trios— something to keep in mind as you select the felt and fabric colors for each. For those of you confident in your skills, the opportunity for customization abounds in this chapter: play with felt and floss colors for different colored plants and pots, use different stitches for leaf patterns, increase or decrease the foliage or add custom text embroidery (page 99).

FREE HUGS CACTUS

While undoubtedly not the cuddliest of plants, cacti sure are cool. Give yours extra character with French knot spines and detached chain blooms. This is one cactus you don't have to worry about getting too close to.

Patterns/Templates: page 159

Stitches: Backstitch (page 19), running stitch (page 19), French knot (page 21) and detached chain stitch (page 21)

Hoop size: 7-inch (18-cm) round

Fabric: 9-inch (23-cm) square of fabric (white)

Felt colors: Dark green

Embroidery floss colors: Black, dark pine green, white and coral

Other materials: Water-soluble fabric pen, fabric scissors, embroidery needle, paper scissors, regular adhesive tape and straight pins

Pattern Transfer Instructions

1. Transfer the Free Hugs text pattern onto your fabric. The text should be centered and offset to the right of the hooped fabric.

2. Hoop the fabric and trim the excess, leaving at least 1 inch (2.5 cm) excess around the entire hoop.

Text Embroidery Instructions

1. With two strands of black thread, work a backstitch over the text. To prevent pulling and visible thread beneath the fabric, backstitch the words separately, and knot the floss and cut off the excess floss before moving on to the next word.

Felt Template Transfer

1. For this project, I transferred each of the templates (#1 through #8) onto the dark green felt in numerical order, and I pinned them into place on the hooped fabric to ensure that every piece lined up properly before the embroidery work.

Embroidery Instructions

1. Starting with template #1 and working in numerical order, embroider a running stitch, using three strands of dark pine green thread, along the perimeter of each felt cactus piece.

2. When the perimeter of each cactus piece is stitched, you are ready to embroider the "spines" of the cactus with French knots. Using four strands of white floss, stitch French knots in a scattered pattern on each of the cactus pieces.

3. To add the cactus' blooms, stitch three detached chains, with three strands of coral thread, extending out from the top of templates #2, #6 and #8.

MONSTERA MADNESS

Monstera deliciosa *is a stunning plant that many, including myself, are simply mad about! Its large, perforated leaves have earned it the charming nickname of the Swiss cheese plant. No chapter of flora-inspired designs would be complete without an ode to its quirky leaves, so here it is: a simple pattern that will "leaf" a big impact on your wall!*

Patterns/Templates: page 161

Stitches: Running stitch (page 19) and backstitch (page 19)

Hoop size: 6-inch (15-cm) round

Fabric: 8-inch (20-cm) square of fabric (peach)

Felt colors: Dark green

Embroidery floss colors: Dark pine green

Other materials: Fabric scissors, paper scissors, regular adhesive tape, straight pins, embroidery needle and water-soluble fabric pen

Hoop the fabric, leaving at least 1 inch (2.5 cm) excess around the entire hoop.

Felt Template Transfer and Embroidery Instructions

1.   Transfer the monstera leaf template onto the dark green felt fabric, and secure it with the straight pins to the hooped fabric. With two strands of dark pine green embroidery thread, work a running stitch along the outside and inside border of the leaf. Use a single strand of the dark pine green thread in a backstitch around the perimeter of the small perforations in the leaf.

2.   Using the dashed line A as a reference, mark the center vein line on the monstera leaf with your fabric pen. Work a backstitch, with two strands of the dark pine green thread, over the marked line.

MUSHROOM TO GROW

It is a little-known fact that gnomes love to make their homes in mushroom stalks. This little mushroom is inhabited by such a gnome who hopes to grow his family. He appreciates all the embroidery work you will do to beautify his mushroom home, and he asks that you find a nice wall with a view for them to hang.

Patterns/Templates: page 163

Stitches: Running stitch (page 19), straight stitch (page 18), backstitch (page 19), French knot (page 21) and detached chain stitch (page 21)

Hoop size: 5-inch (13-cm) round

Fabric: 7-inch (18-cm) square of fabric (pale pink)

Felt colors: Red, white, walnut brown and black

Embroidery floss colors: Red, white, dark brown, black, dark fern green and yellow

Other materials: Fabric scissors, paper scissors, regular adhesive tape, straight pins, embroidery needle, ruler and water-soluble fabric pen

Hoop the fabric, leaving at least 1 inch (2.5 cm) excess around the entire hoop.

Felt Template Transfer and Embroidery Instructions

1. Start by transferring the mushroom cap template (#1) onto the red felt fabric, and transfer the templates for the mushroom gill (#2) and mushroom stem (#3) onto the white felt. Lay out all three transferred pieces on the fabric with the mushroom cap being placed down first. The gill should be placed second and positioned on top of the mushroom cap towards the bottom. The stem is placed down last with the top of the stem overlapping a portion of the gill. Use the Mushroom to Grow picture for placement reference, if needed.

2. When the pieces are laid out to your liking, remove the gill and stem from the fabric. Pin the mushroom cap into place. Work a running stitch, with two strands of red embroidery floss, to embroider the mushroom cap onto the fabric.

3. Pin the gill piece into position on top of the mushroom cap. Stitch it into place using a running stitch with two strands of white floss. Use two strands of white floss to straight stitch the lines of the gills approximately ¾ inch (1.2 cm) apart.

4. Pin the mushroom stem back into place. Work a running stitch with two strands of the white embroidery floss to embroider the stem.

5. Transfer the white spot templates (#4) onto the white felt. Round any sharp edges of the felt with your scissors after you remove the tape. Embroider them onto the mushroom cap using a backstitch, with a single strand of white embroidery floss, following the outline of each spot.

6. Transfer the door and window templates—the door template (#5) onto the walnut brown felt and the window template (#6) onto the black felt. Use a single strand of white floss to backstitch the window into place toward the top of the mushroom stem. Make two vertical backstitches down the center of the window and two horizontal backstitches across the center of the window. With a single strand of the dark brown floss, backstitch three rows vertically onto the door to secure it to the bottom of the stem. Use your single strand of dark brown floss to make a French knot for the doorknob. With two strands of the dark brown floss, make a horizontal straight stitch under the window to create a window ledge. To add a window to the front door, use two strands of black thread and stitch a French knot in the top center of the door.

Grass Embroidery Instructions

1. Remove the fabric from the hoop. Transfer the grass pattern to the fabric so the grass is positioned at the bottom of the mushroom stem with the stem centered. Hoop the fabric. Use two strands of the dark fern green floss to backstitch the grass and flower stem. Make two or three straight stitches on the side of the stem to create the leaf. With two strands of the white floss, create a lazy daisy flower from five detached chain stitches in a circle at the top of the flower stem. Embroider a French knot in the center of the flower with two strands of yellow floss.

POT OF PILEA

A plant as beloved as Pilea peperomioides *(otherwise known as the Chinese money plant) surely needs its own embroidery design. This one is in a glazed planter with a plate. Its bright green pancake-shaped leaves are both adorable and fun to embroider, with a French knot holding each leaf in place in this simple and easy design. Embroider one for yourself and one for a friend—fitting for a plant that spread throughout the world by cuttings being passed between friends!*

Patterns/Templates: page 165

Stitches: Running stitch (page 19), backstitch (page 19) and French knot (page 21)

Hoop size: 5-inch (13-cm) round

Fabric: 7-inch (18-cm) square of fabric (ivory)

Felt colors: Mint, antique white and green

Embroidery floss colors: Mint, bright chartreuse and light green

Other materials: Fabric scissors, paper scissors, regular adhesive tape, straight pins, embroidery needle and water-soluble fabric pen

Hoop the fabric, leaving at least 1 inch (2.5 cm) excess around the entire hoop.

Felt Template Transfer and Embroidery Instructions

1. Begin by transferring the planter template (#1) onto the mint felt fabric, and pin it into place centered towards the bottom of the hoop. Use two strands of mint embroidery floss to make a running stitch along the perimeter of the planter. Next, use your fabric pen to draw the line of the planter's plate at the bottom of the planter. Refer to the dashed line (A) on the planter template (#1) for line placement. Use a backstitch with the two strands of mint floss to embroider over your line.

2. Transfer the glazed planter top template (#2) onto the antique white felt. Mark the opening of the planter by drawing the two lines at the top of the planter. Refer to the dashed lines (B and C) on the template #2 for line placement. The two lines should connect at the outer edge of the planter. Now use a backstitch with two strands of mint floss to stitch along your drawn lines. Finally, with the two strands of mint floss, embroider a running stitch along the jagged edge of the antique glaze.

3. To add the leaves, begin by transferring the leaf templates (#3 through #9) one at a time onto the green felt. The leaves should be transferred and pinned to the hooped fabric in the order shown on the template page. Pin each leaf into place on the hoop before transferring the next leaf to the felt. The embroidery for the leaves is minimal: work a French knot with two strands of the bright chartreuse floss towards the top of each leaf.

4. The last embroidery step for the leaves is to draw and embroider the stems. Begin by marking the center stem which extends from the bottom-center Pilea leaf (#9) to the bottom backstitched line at the top of the pot. All of your other stem lines should connect to this center stem line using a slightly curved line. When your lines are marked, use three strands of the light green floss to backstitch them. Your leaves are only secured into place with a French knot; you can gently lift them without disturbing the knot to draw or embroider the stem lines if needed.

FIDDLE LEAF FIGGY WITH IT

If you follow home décor trends, you know that houseplants are a hot commodity. Fiddle leaf fig trees are especially popular, but they are also notoriously difficult to care for. For a plant that is on trend but requires no care other than the occasional dusting, give this fiddle leaf fig pattern a try! This pattern demonstrates how the split stitch can be used to add visual interest to a piece—in this case, by taking a piece of tan felt and split stitching it into a textured plant basket!

Patterns/Templates: page 167

Stitches: Running stitch (page 19), split stitch (page 20), backstitch (page 19) and straight stitch (page 18)

Hoop size: 5-inch (13-cm) round

Fabric: 7-inch (18-cm) square of fabric (coral)

Felt colors: Tan and green

Embroidery floss colors: Tan, dark brown and white

Other materials: Fabric scissors, paper scissors, regular adhesive tape, straight pins, embroidery needle, water-soluble fabric pen and ruler

Hoop the fabric, leaving at least 1 inch (2.5 cm) excess around the entire hoop.

Felt Template Transfer and Embroidery Instructions

1. Begin by transferring the plant basket template (#1) onto the tan felt fabric, and pin it into place centered at the bottom of the hoop. Use two strands of tan embroidery floss for all of the basket embroidery work. First make three to four running stitches down both sides of the basket to fully secure the felt to the fabric.

2. To create the basket design, use your fabric pen to first mark and then embroider the dashed lines (A through F) shown on the basket drawing on the template page. With two strands of tan floss, split stitch the top horizontal inside line of the basket (A). Your line should follow the curve of the top of the felt basket. Next, split stitch line B. Remember to follow a slight curve that mimics the top and bottom of the felt basket. Repeat the split-stitched curved line four more times for lines C, D, E and F; each line is approximately a ¼ inch (6 mm) apart. The last step for the basket is to split stitch the handles into place at the top of the basket (G): Start at the top outside corners of the basket. Stitch inwards ¼ inch (6 mm) in an upside-down U shape. The last stitch of the U should connect with the second split-stitched line at the top of the basket.

3. Next, use your ruler to mark a 2¾-inch (7-cm) straight line that is centered in the middle of the fabric. The line should start at the second split-stitched line from the top of the basket and extend up towards the top of the hoop. Use six strands of the dark brown embroidery to backstitch the straight line.

4. For the fiddle leaf fig leaves, transfer them onto the green felt. Feel free to lay out your leaves in a pattern of your choosing or follow the example shown in the Fiddle Leaf Figgy With It picture. For a "fuller" tree, transfer the leaf templates multiple times to add additional leaves. In the example shown, the leaves running down the left-hand side of the dark brown stem are, starting from the bottom, #2, #3 and #4. The leaves on the right-hand side of the stem—starting from the bottom—are #5, #6, #7 and #7 again. Overlap some of the leaves for a realistic-look that creates visual interest.

5. To embroider the leaves into place, use a single strand of white embroidery floss to make the veins of each leaf. Start by making a straight stitch down the center of each leaf. Straight stitch two to three lines going downwards diagonally off the center vein line. Repeat on both sides of the center line on each leaf.

SSSNAKE PLANT

Even easier than caring for a real snake plant is caring for an embroidered one! Plant and craft lovers alike will enjoy layering the felt leaves to give their felted plant dimension. And just like a real-life snake plant, this pattern is not fussy. You can layer the leaves to your liking, and the embroidery time is minimal with a straight stitch doing most of the work!

Patterns/Templates: page 169

Stitches: Straight stitch (page 18), running stitch (page 19) and backstitch (page 19)

Hoop size: 5-inch (13-cm) round

Fabric: 7-inch (18-cm) square of fabric (mint)

Felt colors: Coral and green

Embroidery floss colors: Dark green and coral

Other materials: Fabric scissors, paper scissors, regular adhesive tape, straight pins, embroidery needle, water-soluble fabric pen and ruler

---

Hoop the fabric, leaving at least 1 inch (2.5 cm) excess around the entire hoop.

Felt Template Transfer and Embroidery Instructions

1.   Begin by transferring the plant pot template onto the coral felt fabric. Pin the pot into place centered at the bottom of the hoop, but wait to stitch it into place until all of the leaves have been embroidered.

2.   Transfer the snake plant leaves onto the green felt. The template paper will stick to each leaf; do not remove the paper from the leaves until you have them placed into position. For this project, I placed all of the leaves into position first to get a sense of how they would line up and overlap before I removed the template paper and stitched them into place one by one.

3.   To lay them out as shown in the picture, start by placing leaf #6 in the center of the hoop. The pinned plant pot should slightly overlap the bottom of the leaf. Next, place #7 next to #6 on the left-hand side. The bottom of all of the leaves should line up. Place #3 on the right-hand side of #6. Remove the template papers, and pin the three leaves into place. Using two strands of dark green embroidery floss, work a horizontal straight stitch in a zigzag pattern down each of the three leaves. The stitches should be reminiscent of the dark green markings on snake plant leaves so do not worry about achieving a perfect zigzag pattern.

4.   When the first three leaves are embroidered, add leaf #8 slightly overlapping #3 on the left side and pin it into place. Next, pin leaf #5 into position centered in between and overlapping #6 and #3. Add leaf #4 next to #5 on the left-hand side where it will overlap #7 and #6. Pin leaf #2 in place angled slightly outwards at the top and overlapping #7 at the bottom. Use two strands of dark green embroidery floss to embroider the zigzag pattern of straight stitches on #8, #5, #4 and #2. Finish by placing leaf #1 overlapping #2 on the left side, and stitch it into place with the zigzag pattern.

5.   When the leaves are embroidered, use three strands of the coral embroidery floss to embroider a running stitch along the perimeter of the plant pot. To add detail to your plant pot as shown by the dashed lines (A through C) on the pot template, use your fabric pen to mark those lines running vertically down the pot. Mark the line A first followed by lines B and C to help ensure equal spacing. If needed, use a ruler to help ensure straight lines. Use a backstitch to make two large stitches for each of the three lines.

FRESH AS A DAISY

This cheerful daisy pattern demonstrates how French knots can create texture when used as a filling and how the satin stitch can be used to mimic the natural lines of a leaf. With its brightly colored felts, this sweet project will bring sunshine to even the dreariest of days.

Patterns/Templates: page 171

Stitches: Backstitch (page 19), satin stitch (page 20) and French knot (21)

Hoop size: 6-inch (15-cm) round

Fabric: 8-inch (20-cm) square of fabric (light yellow)

Felt colors: White and yellow

Embroidery floss colors: Dark hunter green, yellow and white

Other materials: Water-soluble fabric pen, fabric scissors, paper scissors, regular adhesive tape, straight pins and embroidery needle

Pattern Transfer Instructions

1. Transfer the stem with the leaf pattern onto your fabric.

2. Hoop the fabric, with the stem and leaf offset to the right. Trim the excess, leaving at least 1 inch (2.5 cm) excess around the entire hoop.

Embroidery Instructions

1. With six strands of the dark hunter green embroidery floss, use a backstitch to embroider the stem. To give your stem added dimension, work a horizontal satin stitch using three strands of the dark hunter green thread over the backstitched stem.

2. To embroider the leaf, use the center line running down the leaf as a divider between your stitches. Starting at the top of the right side of the leaf and working down, embroider a satin stitch with three strands of dark hunter green floss. Your stitches should be embroidered using an upwards/outwards slant. When you have the right side of the leaf embroidered, switch to the left side of the leaf using the same upwards/outwards satin stitch. After both sides of the leaf are embroidered, the center line that runs down the leaf mimics the center vein of a leaf.

Felt Template Transfer and Embroidery Instructions

1. Transfer the daisy petals template (#1) onto the white felt fabric. Secure them with the straight pins to the hooped fabric directly above the stem.

2. Next, transfer the center of the daisy (#2) onto the yellow felt, and pin it to the center of the petals. To add visual interest and texture to the daisy, embroider a series of French knots in the yellow felt center of the flower using four strands of yellow thread.

3. Before you embroider the petals of the daisy, use your fabric pen to draw an outline along each petal. The outline for each petal should start at the yellow center of the daisy and extend up and around the curve of each petal. Use the Fresh as a Daisy picture for reference. Embroider a backstitch with two strands of white thread around the marked perimeter of the daisy petals.

make it
PERSONAL

In the following section, I'll provide some tips on how to personalize or customize the projects in this book. These are just ideas to get you started. Remember, with embroidery work, the options for customization abound!

Name or Custom Text Embroidery

One of the simplest ways to personalize a project is to add a name or special phrase to the piece. This might mean substituting a phrase that's already included in the pattern with one of your own or adding a child's name and date of birth to a design. Adding a family's last name or a couple's wedding date are two other ways to make an embroidered gift really stand out!

Whichever personalization option you choose, here are a few tips to help you get started:

Personalized Text Embroidery (name, special dates, etc.)

Begin by cutting the fabric to hoop size as you normally would, leaving at least 2 inches (5 cm) of excess fabric around the border. Be sure you allow space for the personalized text in your design. For example, if you are adding text to an animal pattern, reserve some space underneath or above the animal when you are hooping the fabric. I often like to first hoop my fabric, then transfer the main template to the felt and pin it to the fabric to determine the spacing before I transfer or write my text pattern on the fabric. Before I add personalized text, I remove the fabric from the hoop with the main template still pinned to the fabric.

Next, determine whether you will freehand the text or create a pattern for it. You can create a pattern in one of two ways: by writing it out on a piece of paper or typing it on a computer. Handwritten patterns make for a more personalized touch, while others may enjoy the look of a special typed font.

If you are using a handwritten or typed pattern for the text, transfer it to the fabric using the technique described in the pattern transfer section of the Getting Started chapter (page 12).

If you are going to freehand the text onto the fabric, use a ruler to measure out the spacing. Determining the spacing in advance helps you to choose the correct letter size. To write in a straight line, I use my ruler and fabric pen to lightly mark a straight line within the allotted space. If I'm writing on a curved line, I will often use the edge of another hoop or even a clean salad plate to mark the curved line.

When writing a name or date, I count the letters or numbers to identify which letter or number is in the middle of the name/date. I write that letter or number in the exact center of my allotted space. Then I go back and add in the remaining letters or numbers. If the name or date has an even number of letters or digits, I figure out where the even break is and place that at the center of the line with the even number of letters/numbers on both sides of the break.

Whether you use a sharpened pencil or fabric pen for adding personalized text is up to you. If you're marking with a fabric pen and make a mistake, remember that you will need to start over with a fresh cut of fabric or rinse the pen marks and allow the fabric to dry before proceeding. If you use a pencil, remember to press lightly onto the fabric as erasing pencil marks can mar the fabric. You may want to purchase a fabric eraser, which is designed to remove pencil marks from fabric, before you start this process.

Custom Phrase Embroidery

Many of the patterns in this book include phrases, but don't feel limited to what is included in the pattern. Feel free to substitute with your own phrase to really personalize the design to suit your home or gift recipient. In addition, you can add a custom phrase to a pattern that doesn't have any text.

Adding a custom phrase to a pattern is similar to the process outlined above for personalized text embroidery. You can create a handwritten or typed pattern and follow the pattern-transfer process (page 12), or you can freehand your phrase directly onto the fabric. Because phrases are typically longer than names or dates, you may need to spend more time measuring and marking with your ruler to determine the correct spacing.

Making Faces

Many of the patterns in this book require you to freehand facial features onto characters or animals. My hand-drawn faces are typically kawaii-inspired. Kawaii is a Japanese concept which basically means *cute*, and I've found that it lends itself well to the backstitch embroidery technique (page 19) that I use for most of my faces. You can follow my patterns and pictures as shown or get creative with your facial features. Regardless of which route you take, I recommend measuring out the placement of facial features before you begin drawing them on the felt.

Eyes

I typically mark the placement of the eyes first. This helps me center the nose and mouth, if applicable. Both eyes should be an equal distance from the outside of the face. I draw my kawaii-inspired eyes in one of two ways: a slightly curved upwards line or slightly curved downwards line. I add two or three eye lashes at the outer corner of each eye if a more feminine look is needed.

If you'd prefer a different style eye, you can also use satin stitches to make a round eye shape with or without eyelashes.

Nose

After determining the eye placement, the nose placement is simple: center the nose directly below the two eyes. For animals, I typically draw an upside-down triangle. For people or human-like characters, I draw a small, slightly curved upwards or downwards line.

Mouth

The mouth will be centered below the nose. For animals, I draw a straight line extending down from the point of the upside-down triangle nose. The length of the line depends on the animal and the allotted spaced. At the bottom, the line splits into two, creating the look of a rounded letter W.

For people or other characters, I draw the mouth in the shape of an uppercase U.

tooling around
TOOLS & MATERIALS

If you're new to embroidery, you'll need to begin by gathering the necessary tools and materials. When I was first starting, I found this task to be a bit daunting and a little confusing. Who knew there were so many different types of needles? And why won't every fabric pair well with embroidery work?

In this section, I'll walk you through the items you will need to get started. Each project includes its own supply list. With a better understanding of the tools and materials you'll need as well as a supply list, your visit to your local craft store won't be quite as overwhelming as mine!

Embroidery Hoops

Embroidery hoops consist of an inner ring which rests inside an outer ring. The outer ring has an adjustment screw at the top of the hoop. The screw is used to tighten the outer ring over the inner ring and fabric, securing your fabric firmly into place while you embroider. A properly tightened embroidery hoop allows you to work with even tension, which helps keep your stitches even and your fabric from puckering.

Embroidery hoops come in a variety of sizes, typically ranging from 3 to 12 inches (8 to 30 cm) in diameter. The size of your embroidery hoop is determined by your project. The patterns in this book call for 5-, 6-, 7- or 8-inch (13-, 15-, 18- or 20-cm) hoops.

Most craft supply stores offer two types of embroidery hoops: wood or plastic. I have noticed that many stores are replacing their wood hoops with bamboo. The material you use is entirely up to you, and wood, bamboo or plastic will work well with the patterns featured in this book. I prefer the look and feel of wood or bamboo, so I gravitate towards those for my projects. From an aesthetic standpoint, some designs may pair better with one type of hoop versus another, so take that factor into consideration as well. Vintage hoops can be found, with luck, in thrift stores or on e-commerce websites that feature vintage goods.

When selecting your hoop, pay special attention to the quality of the hoops. Sadly, they are not all of equal quality—sometimes despite being from the same manufacturer. I have noticed this especially in wood hoops. It's common to find a wood hoop that's warped or heavily slivered, and this may distract from your finished embroidery work. In addition, a warped hoop will not hold the fabric properly in place and you may be forced to constantly adjust your fabric as you work.

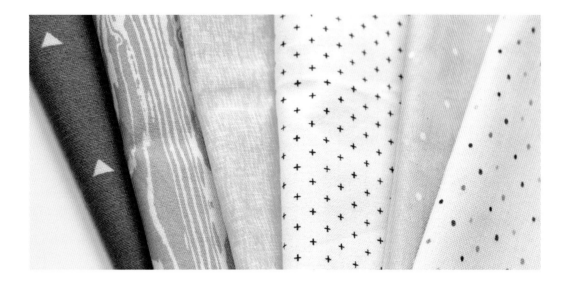

Fabrics

Not all fabric types pair well with embroidery. In general, fabrics with a looser weave, such as cotton, muslin and linen, work best. Your embroidery needle can pass easily through looser weave fabrics, which saves you time and eliminates the discomfort in your fingers and hands that comes from trying to work a needle through a too-tight weave.

One of the best tips I received when I first started was from a store clerk who encouraged me to always feel the fabrics first. After you've gained a better understanding of the fabrics you like to use, you can order fabrics online with greater confidence.

While neutrals or subdued colors are my favorite for embroidery work, I enjoy using both brighter colors and patterns with my projects, too. Keep in mind that your design is the "star of the show" and your fabric selection should enhance and not detract from it. Patterns can be a bit tricky, so I prefer to keep them subtle.

Felt

Choosing felts is one of my favorite parts of any project. There's nothing like a stack of felt fanned out in a rainbow of colors. While choosing felt may not be as challenging as choosing your fabric, there are a few tips and tricks to make the job easier.

If you've never worked with felt, you may be surprised to learn that it can be a bit tricky. It takes some hands-on learning—and some trial and error—to get comfortable with felt.

Type

As you will soon learn, not all felt is created equal. Here's a brief overview of the three most common types of felt with my recommendations for embroidery work:

Wool

Wool felt is made from 100% wool. It is sold by the yard. While it is a beautiful and dense material, it is expensive and I've found that wool-blend or craft felt will suffice for most projects.

Wool-Blend

Wool-blend felt is made from a wool and rayon blend. It's my preferred type of felt for embroidery due to its nice, pliable texture and its wide color selection. Additionally, it holds up well to the template-transfer process and is less likely to pill over time. Wool-blend felt is sold by the yard or in sheets, and it can be purchased at local craft stores, fabric and craft chain stores or online through sites like Benzie Design. While it is more expensive than craft felt, it is still reasonably priced and produces a higher-quality finished product.

Craft Felt

Craft felt refers to 100% synthetic felt that is typically made from acrylic, polyester or rayon. Eco-friendly craft felt falls in the craft felt category, and it is made from 100% post-consumer recycled plastic bottles. Craft felt comes in sheets, and it is available at local craft stores as well as fabric and craft chain stores. Although it's thinner than wool-blend felts and has a limited color selection, it's very affordable and will suffice for some embroidery projects. If you are working with craft felt, please take extra care not to press too hard when transferring templates using tape. Due to its sparse fibers, craft felt is more prone to stretching and distortion during the tape removal process. And remember not to iron craft felt, as the heat will cause it to melt!

Working with Felt

Cutting Felt

Felt differs from other fabrics in that it's too thick to trace a design through for template or pattern transfers with a light source. After several years of trying different methods, my favorite method for cutting felt is with standard clear tape. I've found it to be both an efficient and accurate method. For detailed, step-by-step instructions of the standard tape method, refer to page 13.

When cutting felt, I prefer to use sharp fabric scissors. Paper scissors often will not cleanly cut through wool-blend felt, or they may cause excess stretching and distortion of the felt. While it's nice to work with large fabric scissors for larger sections, I recommend using small fabric scissors as many of these projects require small, detailed cuts.

Craft felt can be a bit tricky to cut due to the sparse fibers which may stretch and pull when cut. I like to keep one hand firmly on the felt close to where I'm cutting while I cut to prevent the felt from moving. It's helpful to turn the felt as you cut it to give yourself greater control over the cuts. A helpful tip for cutting clean circles is to continually turn the felt while you keep your fabric scissors in one spot.

Marking Felt

Felt can also be difficult to mark. If you press too hard, your pen or pencil can accidentally pull the fibers, creating a messy appearance. For light-colored felt, I recommend using a water-soluble fabric pen (page 109). While you want to be careful not to press too hard and disrupt the fibers, fabric pens provide greater room for error as you rinse any visible pen marks at the end of your project.

For darker-colored felt, I like to use a slim piece of white chalk. When using chalk on felt, use a light hand and don't press too hard. If you press hard, it can be difficult to remove the chalk marks from the felt. I don't recommend using colored chalk for marking felt as it can stain the surrounding background fabric.

Pencils can be used to mark felt, but I don't recommend it. It's difficult to remove pencil marks from fabric without a fabric eraser. In addition, erasing pencil marks from felt is very disruptive to the felt fibers, and it gives the felt an unsightly appearance.

Rinsing Felt

If you use a fabric pen for marking on felt, you will need to rinse the felt at the end of your project. After I rinse the fabric and felt, I lay it flat to dry on a clean, hard surface, and I use my clean hand to gently smooth out the felt/fabric. I pay special attention to the felt pieces to ensure that they are laying smooth and flat to dry.

Embroidery Floss (Thread)

Separating Floss Strands

Embroidery floss is typically made up of six strands of cotton thread that can be separated depending on your design needs or pattern instructions. For a thicker, bolder design, use all six strands of thread. For finer, more detailed work, use one to five strands. To separate your strands, cut your desired length of floss for your project. Use your fingernails to gently pull your required number of strands away from the cut section of floss. Gently work your way down the floss, separating the strands as you go. Reserve the remaining threads for later.

Buying and Storing Embroidery Floss

While there are several embroidery floss manufacturers, I use DMC embroidery floss. It's a popular brand that can be found at the major craft and fabric supply stores. It's available in a full rainbow of colors that match most felt fabrics.

There are different means for storing your embroidery floss: floss bobbins, wood clothespins, etc. I typically keep my floss in their skeins and store by color in small containers. I recommend trying different storage options until you find the one that works best for you. It's important to keep your floss organized to avoid wasting time trying to select your desired thread from a pile of mixed-up skeins.

Embroidery Needles

Choosing the correct needles for embroidery work can feel a bit confusing when you're first beginning. Yet finding a good-quality needle in the correct style is essential. A poor-quality needle of the wrong type will work against you, creating unnecessary frustration and potentially damaging your piece.

Embroidery needles are long and thin with a very sharp point that moves easily in and out of fabric suited for embroidery work (refer to page 105 for tips on fabric selection). Embroidery needles have a large hole (eye) at the top for threading your needle (page 17). You can find embroidery needles in your craft supply store next to the embroidery floss.

Embroidery needles are available in a range of numbered sizes: The larger the number, the smaller the needle. Select your needle size based on the fabric you're using as well as the thickness of your thread. Your needle should glide easily through the fabric and felt without having to tug to pull it through, and it should not leave a hole behind after going through the fabric. I recommend purchasing a variety pack of sizes and testing them to see which one feels best in your hand and works well with your fabric and felt.

Straight Pins

Straight pins are a small but necessary tool when doing felt embroidery work. A straight pin is a small, thin pin with a very sharp end that's used to hold fabric in place while sewing, or in this case, embroidering the felt to fabric. Purchase a pack of straight pins as well as a small container to store them. You can find straight pins with the sewing tools in a craft or fabric store.

Water-Soluble Fabric Pens

You will need a good fabric pen for transferring patterns to fabric or marking embroidery details on felt. Water-soluble fabric pens use ink that can be rinsed away with water at the end of your project. They typically come with blue or purple ink; use the color you prefer. Select a fabric pen with a fine point for the patterns in this book as you will need it for drawing out finer details and text. Fabric pens are typically located near the quilting tools in craft and fabric stores. Please read your pen's instructions before use.

Pencils

If you'd prefer to use a pencil, I'd recommend purchasing a fabric eraser, which is typically used by quilters. Be careful when erasing on fabric or felt as the eraser can disturb the fibers. It is difficult to erase pencil marks from felt, so be sure not to press too hard when marking it with a pencil.

Rulers

Last, but certainly not least in terms of use and necessity, is a ruler. Rulers come in handy for marking text placement, drawing straight lines or measuring stitch placement when drawing out faces. Depending on the size of my project, I will work with a standard 12-inch (30-cm) ruler for larger hoops or a 6-inch (15-cm) ruler for smaller hoops. Rulers can be purchased at major chain stores or craft stores. Feel free to purchase a fancy sewing ruler, but a regular ruler will work, too.

Hot Glue Guns

To finish the backs of your projects as described in the Getting Started chapter (page 22), you'll need a glue gun and glue sticks. Hot-temperature glue guns with the corresponding glue sticks work best for wood and fabrics. You can purchase a hot glue gun and glue sticks at any craft supply store.

patterns & FELT TEMPLATES

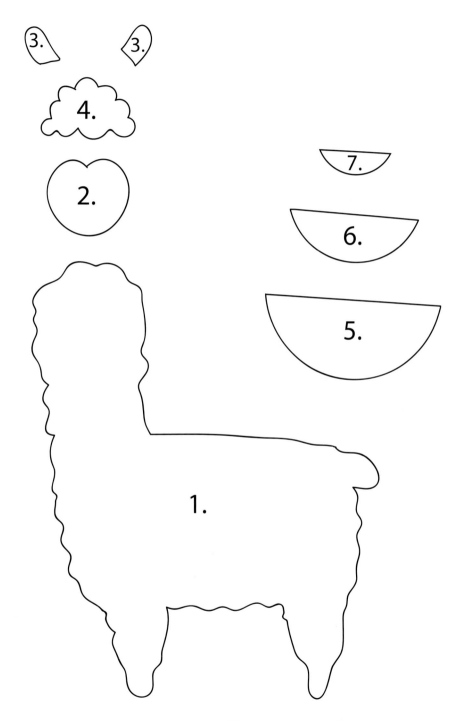

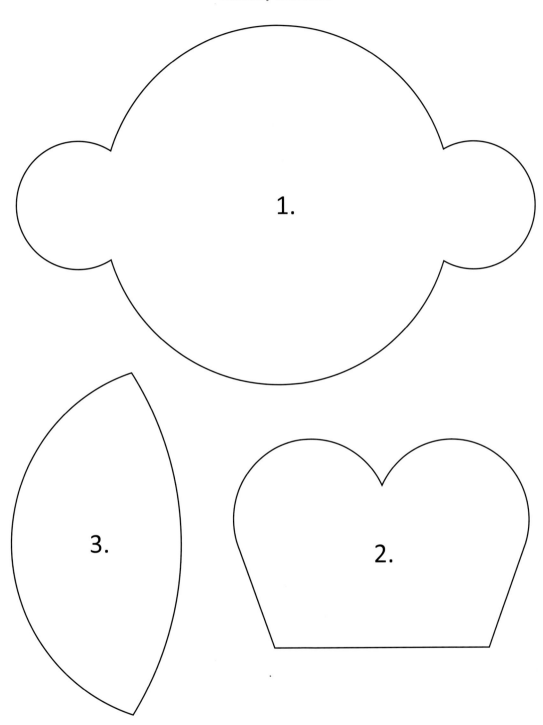

1.

3.

2.

1.

2.

4.

3.

3.

5.

Elephant in the Room

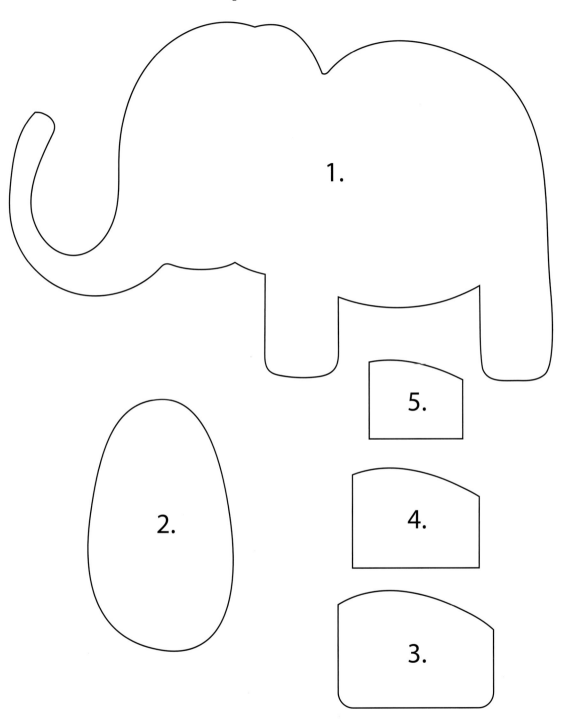

1.

2.

3.

4.

5.

③ 3. ③ 3. ③ 3.

1.

LOVE

BUG

2.

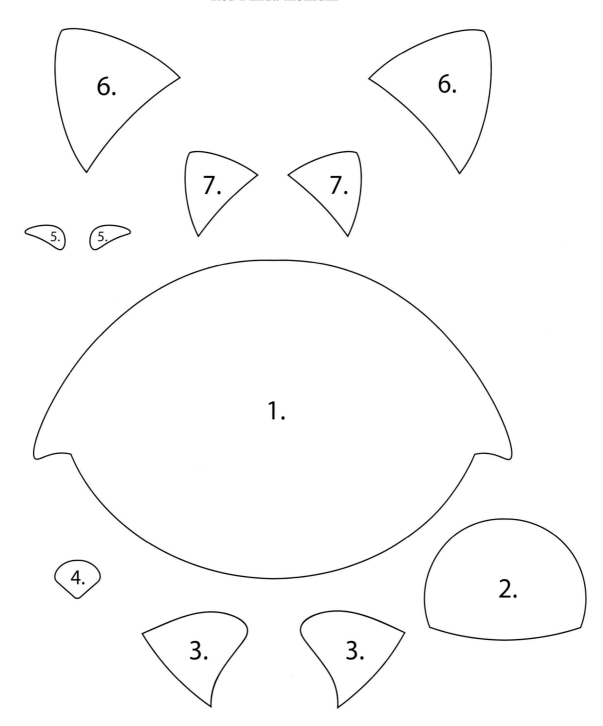

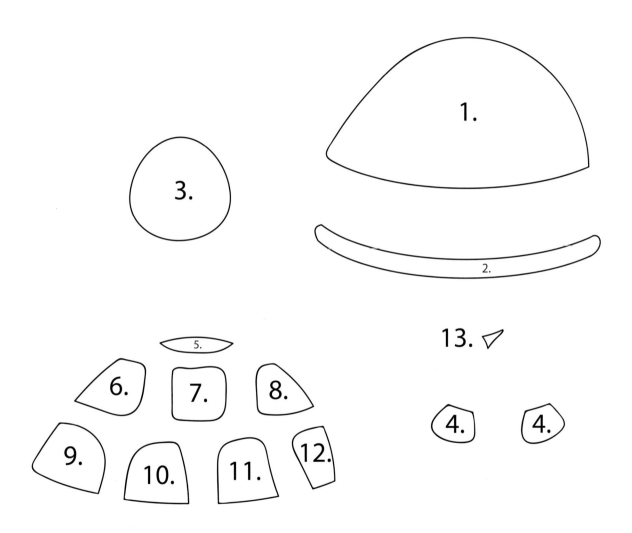

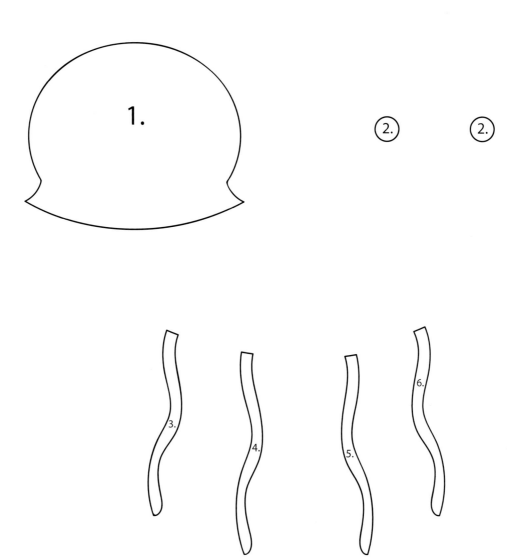

Home is wherever

I'm with you

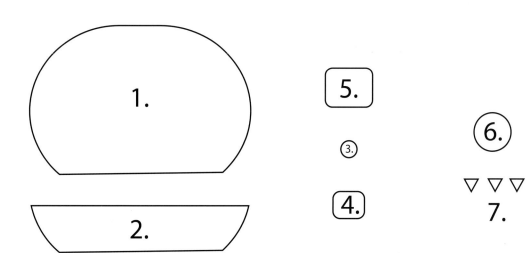

1.

2.

5.

3.

4.

6.

▽ ▽ ▽

7.

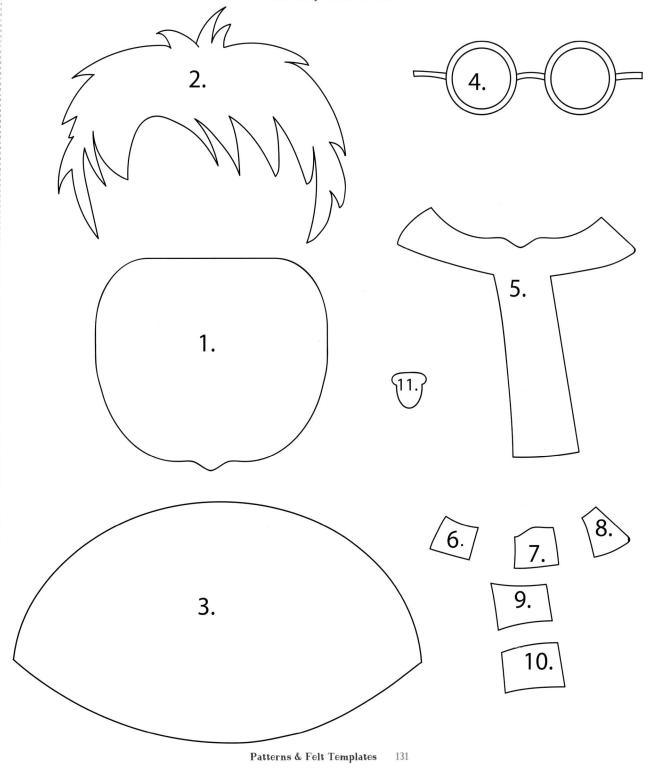

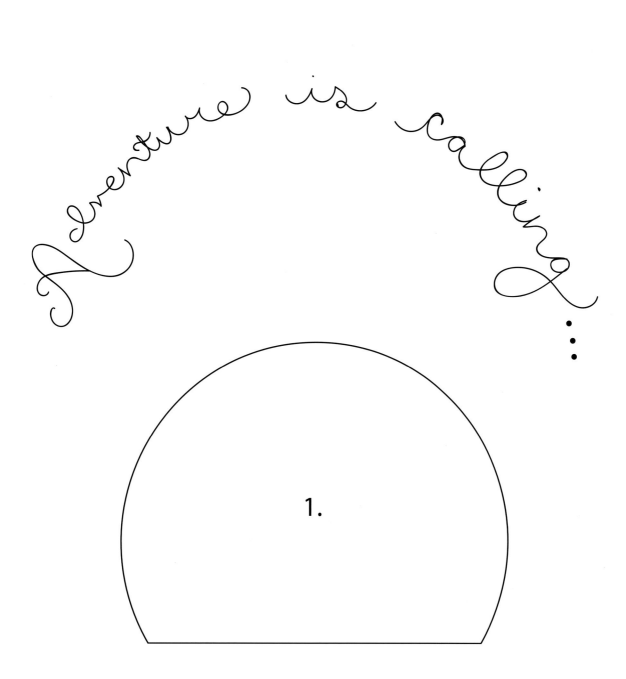

1.

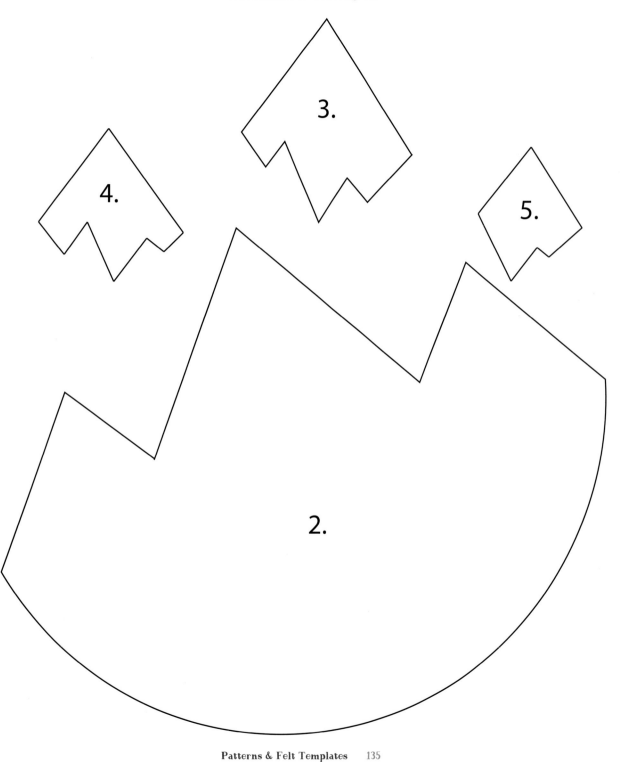

Make a Splash Mermaid

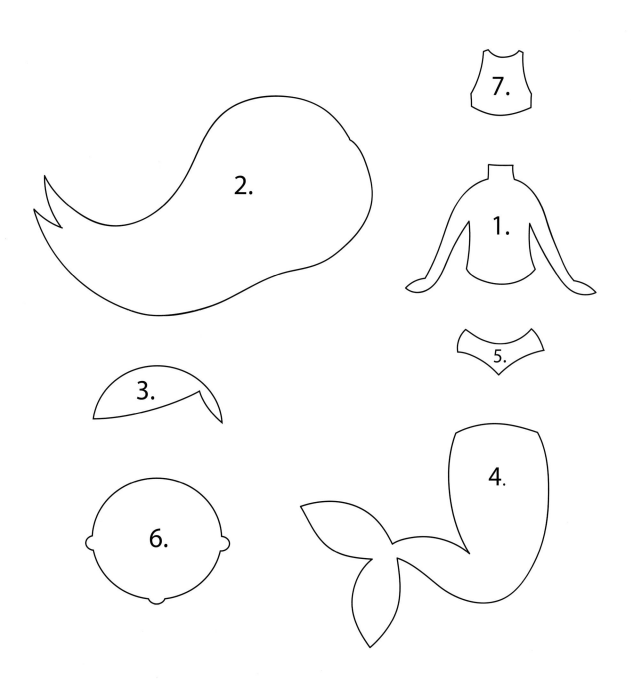

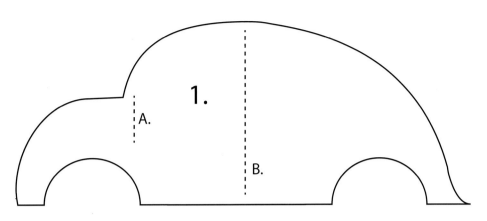

Oh, the places you'll go!

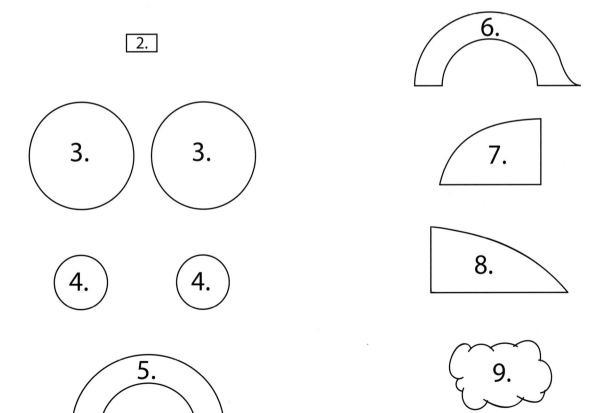

Spaced Out
(Scale up 10%)

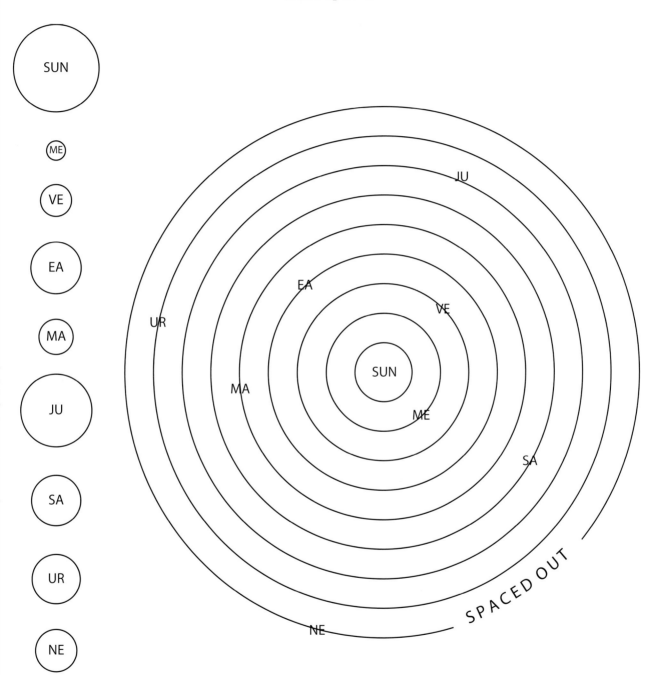

donut worry eat sprinkles

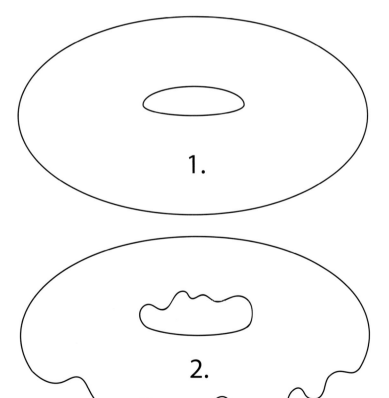

1.

2.

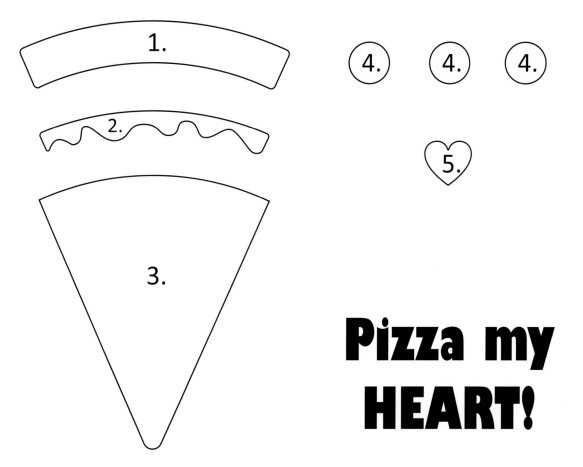

1.

2.

3.

4. 4. 4.

5.

Pizza my HEART!

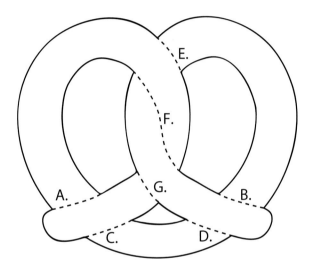

Don't get it twisted.

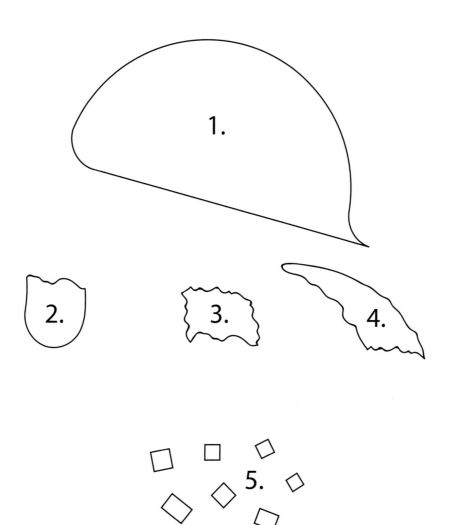

1.

2.

3.

4.

5.

Taco to me.

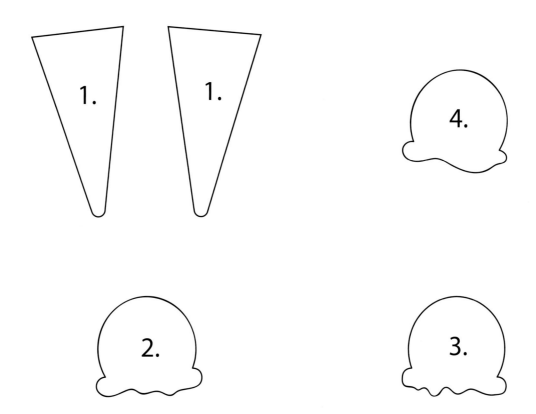

Ice Scream, You Scream!

Love You a Latte!

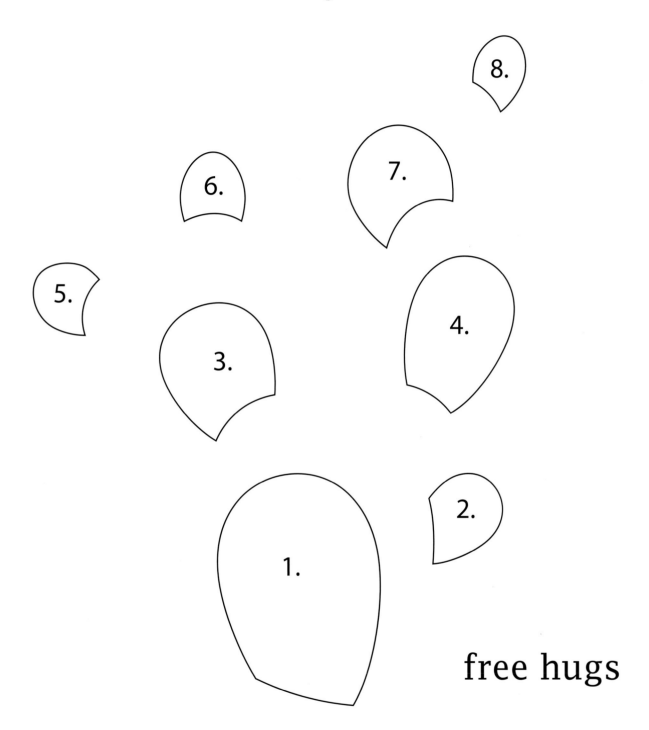

8.

7.

6.

5.

4.

3.

2.

1.

free hugs

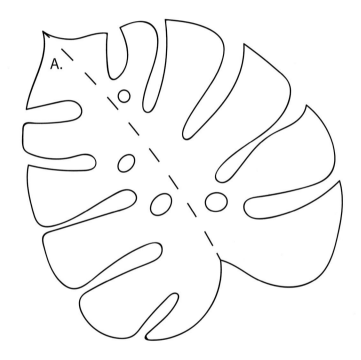

A.

Mushroom to Grow

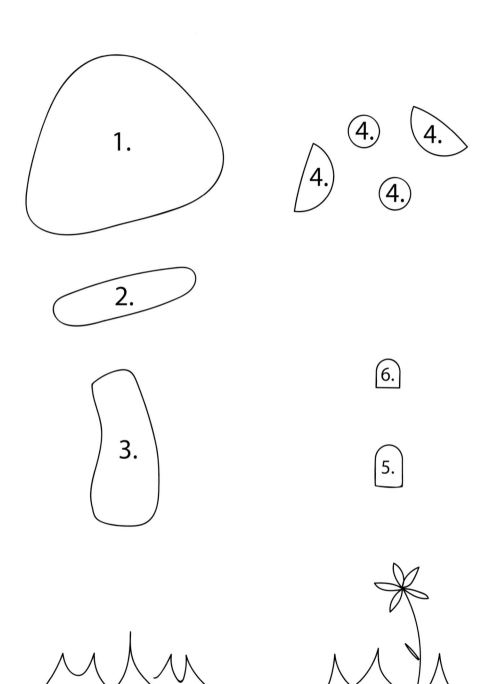

1.

4.

4.

4.

4.

2.

6.

3.

5.

Pot of Pilea

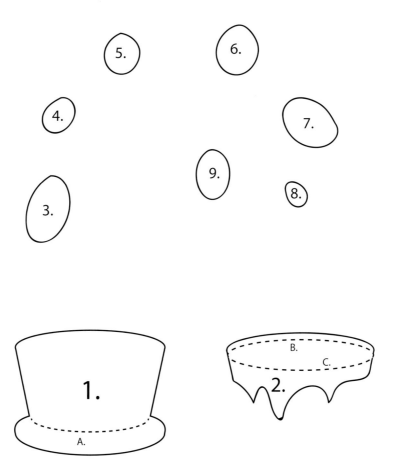

5.

6.

4.

7.

9.

8.

3.

1.

A.

2.

B.

C.

Fiddle Leaf Figgy With It

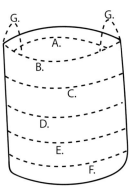

G. G.
A.
B.
C.
D.
E.
F.

*For embroidery reference only—DO NOT CUT

1.

 5.

 3.

 7.

 4.

6.

2.

Sssnake Plant

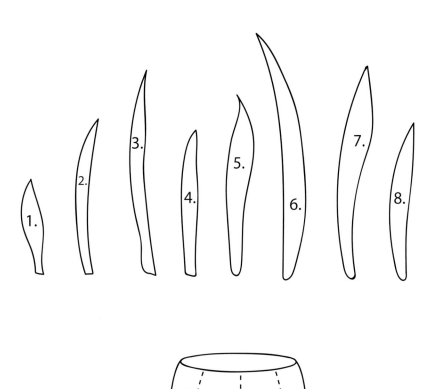

ACKNOWLEDGMENTS

Embroidery expanded my world and for that I'm grateful. To my customers and fellow creatives, thank you for your support and inspiration.

To my editor, Caitlin, and the Page Street team, for guiding me through this process with kindness and respect. For seeing the potential in my work and encouraging me to share it in book form.

To my mom, Sandy, for your unwavering support through it all. To my dad, Doug, for all the nights we read bedtime stories that helped lay the foundation for my creative mind.

To my love, Chris, for being my partner and best friend for almost twenty years. For doing the hard work together—to run our businesses, nurture our family and build our marriage. This dream of writing a book is infinitely more beautiful because we did it together.

And last, but definitely not least, to my children, Milo and Olive. You are my heart, my dreams, my loves. Your births made me rediscover the girl I'd long forgotten. She existed in a world of fairy tales, unicorns and talking animal friends. When I had you both, I found her again. And for that, I'm forever blessed.

ABOUT THE AUTHOR

Meghan is the owner and creative behind the Etsy shop Olive & Fox. You can follow her work on Instagram @oliveandfox. Meghan lives in Minneapolis, Minnesota, with her husband, Chris, their two children and a menagerie of pets. Together they enjoy exploring the outdoors, eating donuts and having dance parties before bed.

INDEX

A

Adventure Is Calling project
  instructions, 56
  templates, 133, 135
Auburn Hoops, 59, 63

B

Backing fabric, 22–23
Backstitch
  instructions for making, 19
  projects using, 28, 31, 32, 35, 36, 39, 40–42, 43–45, 46,
    50–52, 53–55, 56, 59, 60, 63, 64, 67, 75, 76, 79, 80, 85,
    86, 89, 90, 93, 94, 97
Bee Kind project
  instructions, 32–33
  templates, 115
Braided texture, 20

C

Cactus project, 85, 159
Chinese money plant, 90–91
Craft felt, 106
Curved lines, stitches for, 19, 20
Custom phrase embroidery, 100

D

Daisy project, 96–97, 171
Dashed lines, 19, 60, 64, 75, 86, 90, 94
Dates, personalizing a project with, 99–100
Detached chain stitch
  instructions, 21
  projects using, 31, 36, 63, 85, 89
Dino-Roar project
  instructions, 60–61
  templates, 139
Don't Be a Jealous Jellyfish project
  instructions, 46
  templates, 127
Don't Get It Twisted Pretzel project
  instructions, 74–75
  templates, 151

Donut Worry project
  instructions, 70–71
  templates, 147
Drying fabric, 22

E

Elephant in the Room project
  instructions, 36–37
  templates, 119
Embroidery floss
  buying and storing, 108
  separating strands, 17, 108
  threading your, 17
Embroidery hoop(s)
  finishing the, 22–23
  properly tightened, 104
  selecting a, 104
Embroidery needles, 17, 108–109
Embroidery stitches. See individual types of stitches
Eyes, 101

F

Fabric(s). See also Felt fabric
  backing, 22–23
  hooping the, 14–16
  rinsing and drying the, 22
  selecting, 105
Fabric eraser, 109
Fabric pens, 12, 109
Faces, making, 100–101
Felt fabric
  marking, 107
  rinsing, 107
  template transfer process, 13
  type of, 105–106
  working with, 106
Felt template transfer, 13
Fiddle Leaf Figgy with It project
  instructions, 92–93
  templates, 167

Filling in shapes, satin stitch for, 20
Finishing your hoop, 22–23
Free Hugs Cactus project
    instructions, 84–85
    templates, 159
French knot stitch
    instructions, 21
    projects using, 28, 32, 35, 36, 39, 43–45, 50–52, 56, 59, 63,
        85, 89, 90, 97
Fresh as a Daisy project
    instructions, 97
    templates, 171

H
Happy Camper hoop, 50
Harry Potter project
    instructions, 53–55
    templates, 131
Home Is Wherever I'm with You project
    instructions, 50–52
    templates, 129
Hoop. See Embroidery hoop(s)
Hooping fabric, 14–16
Horizontal stitch, 50, 89
Hot glue gun, 23, 109

I
Ice Scream, You Scream project
    instructions, 79–80
    templates, 155

J
Jellyfish project, 46–47, 127

K
Kawaii-inspired faces, 100
Knots, 17, 18

L
Ladybug project, 38–39, 121
Latte project, 80–81, 157
Letters, satin stitch for filling in, 20. See also Text
    embroidery
Light source, for pattern transfer, 12
The Little Mermaid, 59

Llama Love project
    instructions, 28–29
    templates, 111
Love Bug project
    instructions, 38–39
    templates, 121
Love You a Latte project
    instructions, 80–81
    templates, 157

M
Make a Splash Mermaid project
    instructions, 59
    templates, 137
Monkey Business project
    instructions, 31
    templates, 113
Monstera deliciosa plant project
    instructions, 86
    template, 161
Mouths, 101
Mushroom to Grow project
    instructions, 89
    templates, 163

N
Names, personalizing a project with, 99–100
Needle, threading the, 17
Noses, 101

O
Oh, the Places You'll Go project
    instructions, 64
    templates, 143
Olive & Fox (Etsy shop), 9, 49
Outdoors, design inspired by, 56
Outlining, stitches for, 19, 20

P
Panda project, 40–42, 112
Pattern transfers, 12
Pencils, 109
Personalized text embroidery, 99–100. See also Text
    embroidery
Phrases, 100

Pig project, 34–35, 117
Pilea peperomiodes plant project, 90–91, 165
Pizza My Heart project
 instructions, 72
 templates, 149
Plastic embroidery hoops, 104
Pot of Pilea project
 instructions, 90
 templates, 165
Pretty in Pig project
 instructions, 35
 templates, 117
Pretzel project, 74–75, 151

Q
Quilting fabric, 22

R
Red Panda-monium project
 instructions, 40–42
 templates, 123
Rinsing the fabric, 22
Rulers, 109
Running stitch
 instructions, 19
 projects using, 28, 31, 32, 35, 36, 39, 40–42, 43–45, 46,
  50–52, 53–55, 56, 59, 60, 64, 67, 71, 72, 75, 76, 79, 80,
  85, 86, 89, 90, 93, 94

S
Satin stitch
 explained, 20
 projects using, 28, 31, 36, 39, 63, 71, 72, 79, 97
Snake plant project
 instructions, 94
 templates, 169
Solar system project, 66–67, 145
Spaced Out project
 instructions, 67
 templates, 145
Split stitch
 instructions, 20
 projects using, 28, 36, 93
Stitch, beginning and ending a, 18. See also individual types
  of stitches

Storage
 embroidery floss, 108
 templates, 13
Straight pins, 109
Straight stitch
 explained, 18
 projects using, 32, 35, 36, 40–42, 43–45, 46, 50–52, 59, 64,
  67, 71, 72, 75, 76, 79, 89, 93, 94
Synthetic felt, 106

T
Taco to Me project
 instructions, 76
 templates, 151
Tape method, 13
Templates, 12–13, 111–171
Text embroidery, 32, 39, 50, 56, 60, 63, 64, 71, 72, 75, 76, 79,
  80, 85, 99–100
Text, stitches used for creating, 19, 20
The Boy Who Lived project
 instructions, 53–55
 templates, 131
Threading the needle, 17
Turtle-Y Cute project
 instructions, 43–45
 templates, 125

W
Washi tape, 12
Water-soluble fabric pen, 12, 109
Wood embroidery hoops, 104
Wool-blend felt, 106
Wool felt, 106

Y
You Are Loved project
 instructions, 62–63
 templates, 141